Disaster
Emergency
Communications

Planning Essentials
Emergency Response Guide
and
Technical Reference

Third Edition

2015

Bascombe J. Wilson, CEM

Disaster Emergency Communications

Planning Essentials
Emergency Response Guide
and
Technical Reference

Third Edition

by
Bascombe J. Wilson, CEM
WØAIR

Published by
DisasterCom World Press
P.O. Box 797
Longmont, Colorado 80502
USA

www.disasters.org

Printed in the United States of America

ISBN: 978-0-615-58702-8

This Book Provides

Communications Planning Tools
Emergency Communications Strategies
Practical Solutions
Technical References

This Book Is For

Emergency Managers
Contingency Planners
Communications Professionals
Police, Fire, EMS and other Public Safety Personnel
Policy Makers and Elected Officials
Volunteers
Amateur Radio Operators, RACES and ARES Teams
International Disaster Response Teams
Recovery Managers
Emergency Management Educators and Students

Dedication

This book is dedicated to the memory of wireless pioneers—including my father—whose fascination with the mysteries of the airwaves led to discoveries, inventions and applications that affect nearly every aspect of living today. Through their vision, curiosity, dedication and hard work, everything we think of as modern communications was made possible.

Acknowledgements

Kathryn Dunlevy-Wilson continues to bring an endless stream of good into my life. She is my most cherished friend and trustworthy partner. She has been my unwavering inspiration for over three decades of marriage. As a journalist, literature professor, editor and author, Kathryn is a walking reference library on everything I have needed to know about research and writing. What good you may find in this book is due to her encouragement, objectivity, critical thinking, and determination that things be done properly. Any errors, of course, should be blamed on the scoundrel Alan Smithee, wherever he is currently hiding.

Kevin J. Dunlevy-Wilson consistently sets a high benchmark of excellence, dedication to the human cause and principled action in all he does. He is a source of constant inspiration to me. I thank him for his friendship, intellectual support and continuing labors as a tireless proponent of justice and democracy.

My late friends Joseph L. Mullinax, David H. Minton, Claude Baker, Alan Christensen, and Daniel Kirby provided me with years of mentorship in disaster emergency communications, while Samuel Cullers introduced me to the nuances and Gordian complexities of international operations. This world is a much finer place because of their vision, dedication and compassion. While I miss them terribly, they live on through the works of new generations that they inspired.

Robert Dockery, Sri S. Suri, Paul Folmsbee, Dennis O'Quinn and Timothy Grogan continue to show me the human side of communications, while never backing down from the most challenging technical and organizational issues.

I am especially grateful to Dennis Fisher, Dennis Harden, Patricia Sarin, Robert Schroder, Larry VanDyke, Mike Lynk, Dennis Huntley, Dan Roberts, Lee Champagne, Dr. Patricia Hooper, Dan Hawkins, Steve Cochrane, Pete Bakersky, Jack Ciaccia, Doug Reneer and Jerry VeHaun for their friendship, professional guidance and thoughtful insight which helped to shape my research for this book.

With deep appreciation, I thank Howard Pierpont, Chair, and the Board of Directors of DERA—The International Association for Preparedness and Response (**www.disasters.org**) for approving publication of this work by DisasterCom World Publications.

Lastly, I want to thank you personally for considering the thoughts offered in this study, and ask that you make future editions more useful through your critical review, feedback and suggestions, which will always be welcome. Please let me hear from you anytime. My email address is: b.j.wilson@disasters.org

Best Wishes,

- Jay

Bascombe J. Wilson
Denver, Colorado

CONTENTS

Acknowledgements   iii

Introduction   1

Background   5

Common Challenges   8

PART ONE: PLANNING ESSENTIALS   11

Planning Overview   13
  Planning Challenges   16
  Basic Considerations   17

Baseline Needs Assessment   19
  Critical Missions   20
  Essential Support Activities   24
  Critical Mission Communications Requirements   27

Assessing the Current System   29
  Communications Flow Analysis   31
    Primary Communications Systems   41
    Backup Communications Systems   43
    Auxiliary Communications Systems   45
    Emergency Communications Systems   47
  Hazard and Threat Identification   49
  Credible Threat Identification   51
  System Impact Analysis   52
  Synergistic Impact Analysis   53
  Overall Risk Assessment   54
  Vulnerability Analysis   56

Gap Analysis   57
  Capability Needs Assessment   57
  Needs vs Existing Capability   57

Strategic Planning   58
  Target Capability List   58
  National Interoperability Goal   59
      60
  Interoperability Self-Assessment Notes   61

Contingency Planning   62
Tactical Planning   63
Tactical Gap Analysis   64
Tactical Deficiencies   64
Detailed Tactical Planning   64
Standard Operating Procedures (SOPs)   65
Field Operations Guides   66
Emergency Resource Lists   67
Mutual Aid Agreements   68
Self-Healing Systems   69
Built-In Redundancy   70
Hot, Warm, Cold Backups   71
Auxiliary Communications Resources   72

PART TWO: EMERGENCY RESPONSE GUIDE   73

Managing the Unexpected   75
Unplanned Emergency Communications   75

Systems Failure and Restoration   76
Assessing the Current Situation   77
Initial Damage Assessment   77
Determining Immediate Resource Needs   78
Prioritizing Resource Requirements   79
Ordering and Managing Resources   80
Your Emergency Communications Plan   81
ICS 205: Sample Incident Radio Communications Plan   82
ICS 205: Blank Incident Radio Communications Plan   83

Emergency Communications Systems   84
Emergency Communications Systems Comparison   84

Emergency Resources   86
Wireline Carriers   87
Wireless Carriers   88
Internet Service Providers   89
Mobile or Portable Satellite Service Providers   90
Government Emergency Telecommunications Service (GETS)   91
Wireless Priority Service (WPS)   92
Telecommunications Service Priority (TSP)   93
Mobile or Portable Repeaters   94
Military Auxiliary Radio System (MARS)   95
Shared Resources High Frequency Program (SHARES)   96

Civil Air Patrol (CAP) 97
Coast Guard Auxiliary 98
Amateur Radio Auxiliary Communications 99
Communications Equipment Manufacturers 100
Communications Equipment Rental 101
Portable Emergency Power Generator Rental 102
Fuel Delivery Services 103
Tower Repair and Climbing Services 104

PART THREE: TECHNICAL REFERENCES 105

Computer Connectors: RS-232 107

Computer Cables: RJ-45 Connections 108

Telephone Plug Standards 109

Telephone Frame Room Standards 110

Glossary 111

International Issues 127

USA-Specific Issues 128
U.S. Radio Frequency Allocation Table 129

APPENDICES 131

Field Operations Guides 133
National Interoperability Field Operations Guide (NIFOG) 133
Auxiliary Interoperability Field Operations Guide (AUXFOG) 133
Amateur Radio Public Service Communications Manual 133

Bibliography 135

Index 149

Final Thoughts 153

About DERA 157

About the Author 159

Introduction

Why a book on Disaster Emergency Communications, and why so much emphasis on technical preplanning?

The simple answer is that few things are more essential to public safety and welfare. Communications systems essential for public safety have become so complex and so interdependent that when parts of the system begin to fail during a disaster, cascading effects are often catastrophic. Only through comprehensive systems analysis and extensive contingency planning is it possible to ensure uninterrupted communications during disaster situations.

No longer are communications systems simple enough for non-technical description. Emergency managers often find themselves in critical decision-making situations with little time to assess technical information and less opportunity to study alternatives. Technicians who do understand components of the system may not have a view of operational requirements outside their field of specialty, and frequently are not in key decision-making positions during emergencies.

The purpose of this book is to present in one reference volume the most critical tools needed for effective emergency communications planning along with a contingency guide and quick reference source so that emergency managers and technicians can better prepare for and respond to disaster situations.

If you have ever experienced what it means to be in charge of a critical operation only to lose communications at the worst possible time, then you know clearly why emergency communications planning is one of the most important areas for community leaders and emergency managers to emphasize. The process is entirely too critical to be left simply to technicians, yet meaningful planning cannot be accomplished without in-depth technical understanding.

Some may question the term "Disaster Emergency Communications," so a word of explanation is in order. In this book—and increasingly throughout the emergency management profession-- *Disaster Emergency Communications* is taken to mean communications and information resources that are mobilized in time of extreme emergency, augmenting normal capabilities or replacing failed systems.

In most industrialized nations, established public safety communications systems are usually designed to handle the biggest events a community expects to experience; however, there are always capacity limits and system vulnerabilities which can cause extreme disruption during a crisis. As recent disasters have shown, the impact of catastrophic events can overwhelm even the most robust and well-planned system.

Developing nations have an even greater challenge, as communications systems often do not adequately support day-to-day needs.

In reality, every community in the world is at some risk of an event that so overwhelms its ability to respond that no other word describes the situation other than "disaster." During a disaster, normal response systems and local resources are usually not sufficient to deal with the situation; very often, primary communications systems begin to fail or slow down due to overload, even if they are not damaged directly.

Communications failures compound all other problems.

This book aims to provide tools that you can use to better prepare for communications emergencies, make effective decisions during crisis, obtain outside help when needed, and start the recovery process.

In the U.S., Canada and Western Europe, as examples, there are major national programs currently underway to dramatically improve public safety communications. This book is not intended to take the place of nor detract from such national and regional/state/provincial initiatives, but rather to supplement those programs with additional planning tools and resources, while at the same time adding a global perspective to the challenge of disaster emergency communications.

This book is intended to help everyone—government officials, business executives, volunteer groups, international organizations, and private individuals—whether technical or not, to better prepare for and deal with communications emergencies.

"In battles, as verbal communication cannot be heard clearly, cymbals and drums are used as commands. Banners and flags are used as signals. At night, use torches and drums.

"If commands are not clear and distinct, if orders are not thoroughly understood, the general is to blame."

Sun Tzu
The Art of War, about 500 B.C.

Background

Without effective communications, it is impossible for any team to work together, or for any leader to exercise direction and control.

Communications failures often have tragic consequences.

> The world's worst civil aviation disaster occurred on March 27, 1977, when two Boeing 747 jumbo jets collided on the runway at an airport on the island of Tenerife, killing 583 people and badly injuring all 64 survivors. The cause? Communications failure; yet investigators found that all radio systems were working exactly as designed.

> Pilots of both aircraft were highly experienced senior airline captains. One was taxiing with permission on the runway, disoriented in heavy fog, and the other misunderstood a radio transmission from the control tower, falsely believing he had been given clearance for takeoff. Many communications factors contributed to this tragedy: Garbled and overlapping radio transmissions, differences in accents among a native Portuguese tower controller, Dutch and American pilots, and exchange of extraneous information that acted as communications noise in one cockpit and use of non-standard terminology by several parties. Muffled microphones. Overlapping transmissions. Radio interference. Until an instant before the tragic fireball, everyone involved felt that they had communicated properly and had understood what they heard.

> Five hundred and eighty three caskets and 64 survivors scarred for life prove that somehow communications failed.

Please don't make the mistake of thinking this historical example doesn't apply to public safety communications today. Workers in every command post, communications room and dispatch center in the world contend with similar challenges daily, as do the response teams on the other end of the circuits.

If you have any doubt how relevant and urgent this topic is, pick up any copy of a public safety journal or professional magazine in a fire department and you will likely find a report of a recent tragedy that resulted from communications failure and misunderstanding, sometimes even when all the electronic components were working as designed.

Human factors combine with component failure, design limitations, channel overload, ambiguous or misdirected messages, interference and systems incompatibility to set the stage for terrible consequences. For example, investigators concluded that many emergency responders perished on 9/11 in the World Trade Center because they did not receive the evacuation order transmitted over their radio networks, and that fourteen firefighters died on Colorado's Storm King Mountain in part because a weather message was not clearly understood and taken into account by command officers. Whether the cause of communications breakdown is technical or human, vulnerabilities need to be carefully studied and safeguards built into critical systems to reduce the probability of failure.

Every day, emergency responders find themselves unable to call for help because they are in the "dead zones" of their systems or they can't talk with other responders because of equipment incompatibility. Even in the best designed public safety radio systems, 90-95% coverage is often considered the maximum coverage that it is affordable to achieve. That's when everything is working normally. Add a disaster scenario and it becomes clear that few priorities are more important than comprehensive planning for emergency communications.

As one frustrated public official famously put it, "Failures of infrastructure, high-impact accidents, natural disasters and terrorist attacks all carry risks of extreme danger that can only be mitigated by the receipt of timely, accurate information…While part of the immediate challenge is technological, the main impediments, it turns out, have to do--not with wires or electromagnetic fields,--but with judgment, responsibility and fear of potential consequences." (Stringer, 2007). He was talking not just about the need for emergency responders to talk among themselves, but to clearly communicate with the public as well.

That official highlighted a critical point: Planners often think of communications systems in technical terms, focusing on equipment specifications and complex electronic issues in isolation from human components, including the public that we ultimately intend to serve. Technical considerations are critically important, but to fully understand communications systems and ways of making them more effective and less susceptible to failure, it is necessary to start with consideration of how information gets transferred from one point to another, and how the message gets processed, validated, interpreted and acted upon.

It is not sufficient, as Sun Tzu warned, simply for a message to be sent. It must be received, interpreted correctly, and acted upon properly. If not, the system has failed and the person in charge is ultimately responsible.

There is a whole field of science devoted to the study of communications theory with an extensive volume of literature dealing with its implications. For our purposes we can simply begin with something that the great American philosopher Yogi Berra once said: "It was impossible to get a conversation going because everybody was talking too much."

Doesn't that describe precisely the chaos most of us have personally experienced at some stage during a crisis?

Put simply, critically important messages get lost or misinterpreted in the noise and chaos, and sometimes the results are tragic. Even worse, if that is possible, is when systems fail to the extent that there is absolute silence.

Common Challenges

Communications failures and operational challenges generally involve one or more of the following situations:

1. Systems failed or slowed down when overloaded.
2. The event causing the disaster also damaged critical communications systems, compounding the problems of response.
3. Systems were not designed to allow the degree of interoperability required by the situation.
4. The amount of message traffic overloaded the information processing capabilities and the decision-making process.
5. Some of the most important information needed by decision makers was unknown and could not be obtained through available sensor systems.
6. Critical information was misrouted or delayed in queue.
7. Feedback was ineffective or misdirected.
8. Message content was frequently misunderstood.
9. Failed systems took a very long time to replace or rebuild.
10. Highly complex systems had single-nodes of failure that did not become apparent until failure actually occurred.
11. Users did not fully understand the strengths and weaknesses of their systems.
12. Designers of systems were not available to assist during emergency response.
13. Systems were sometimes designed without regard to what the users really need.
14. Prolonged electrical power outages led to failure of communications and information technology systems when backup power systems failed to operate or exhausted their fuel supplies.
15. Systems were vulnerable to sabotage.
16. Systems were so dependent on proprietary technology from certain vendors that repairs, workarounds and upgrades were either impossible or seriously constrained.
17. Budget constraints, political pressures or outside influences led to imbalanced tradeoffs between system operability, reliability, sustainability, security and interoperability.
18. Valid system requirements exceeded budget availability and the resulting system did not meet user needs.

Taking a lesson from the mishap investigation process, we can generalize that the cause of a communications system failure can be traced to one or more of the following:

- Planning Failure
- Technical Failure
- Procedural Failure
- Training Failure
- Personal Failure

You may have to deal with one or more of these issues alone or in combination, and you may face additional, unique challenges. You will find some helpful planning strategies in the section that follows, but first, let's put all this in context.

At one time, sales staffs were taught that customers usually could be offered a choice between three features with any product or service: *High Quality, Quick Delivery and Low Price*. The customer could choose any two, but never could they have all three at once.

> High quality and low price would take longer to deliver

> Quick delivery and high quality would be very expensive

> Low price and fast delivery would result in low quality

In most cases, the tradeoff among those three options proved to be true, whether you were talking about building airplanes, training students, or having a suit tailored. In planning modern communications systems, the equation has become much more complex, as the key options include:

Capability
Reliability
Flexibility
Usability
Deliverability
Maintainability
Security
Interoperability
Restorability
Affordability

No system ever devised has been able to maximize all these features at once. For example, a system that is universally interoperability might make some security compromises. A system with ultimate flexibility might be difficult to use. A system promising to do everything might not actually be deliverable or affordable. A low-cost system probably skimps on everything.

Unfortunately for emergency managers and communications planners, outside influences often dictate emphasis on one or more of these features at the cost of others which ultimately may be even more important during an emergency.

The end result is that every practical communications system is an amalgamation of compromises, some desirable and some painful. Disaster emergency communications planners, therefore, must deal with systems as they are, identify strategies to mitigate weaknesses, and develop contingency plans to respond to potential failures.

In the analysis and planning pages that follow in Part One, strategies will be presented for dealing with each of these challenges and you will have the opportunity to identify and document the unique issues your organization faces.

Illustration: Shutterstock

"The single biggest problem in communication is the illusion that it has taken place."

- George Bernard Shaw

Part One: Planning Essentials

Planning Overview

The aim of the planning process is, of course, to establish the basis for sound decision making and—in the case of communications systems—to devise an infrastructure layout that meets user requirements while being as resistant to failure as is practical. It's often said that the planning process is more important than the plan itself, and while there may be truth in that concept, the end result of communications planning needs to be a system that works, not just a plan on the shelf or a set of good intentions.

Achieving that end result takes vision, time, diligence, interagency cooperation, strategy and trust in addition to technical expertise.

In general, successful planning depends on a series of steps:

1. Agreement by senior leadership on overall goals and processes
2. Identification of all direct and indirect stakeholders in the process
3. Outreach to stakeholders and identification of their interests
4. Agreement by stakeholders on objectives including timelines and responsibilities
5. Identification and analysis of needs, desires, risks, vulnerabilities, strengths, weaknesses and opportunities
6. Technical assessments and cost-benefit analysis of alternatives
7. Consensus among stakeholders as to best course of action
8. Regular dialogue with senior leadership to ensure support
9. Adherence to a definite but not an overly inflexible planning and implementation timeline
10. A dedicated but realistic planning leader or leadership team
11. Drafting and approval of the final plan
12. Funding for the plan
13. Complete accountability to those ultimately in charge

Almost anyone can lock themselves in a quiet room and write a plan that looks good.

Almost any communications consultant can draft an impressive looking blueprint for a radio system and information technology scheme without ever talking with actual users.

Unfortunately, many fill-in-the-blank documents and boiler-plated plans accomplish little more than either of those two approaches.

The communications planning approach that follows is intended to help you do much more than produce a boiler-plate plan. Whether you are conducting the planning for a community, a business, a nonprofit organization, or even a state, region or nation, this part of the book should help you organize your efforts, structure your analysis, and guide your planning team's work.

Disaster emergency communications are often thought of as the ad-hoc resources that are mobilized after the disaster when primary systems have failed. While in a sense that is true, it is also possible to start at the beginning of the communications planning process and build in as much resilience, redundancy and recoverability as feasible, clearly identify remaining weaknesses, and preplan your needs for disaster emergency communications to fill in the unavoidable gaps. With that goal in mind, the following planning process outlines a comprehensive approach for planning new communications systems or reviewing the ones you now have while identifying the gaps that will need disaster emergency communications contingency support.

To start the process, it is recommended that you set up a system of planning documentation that includes the following categories as a minimum:

1. Applicable laws and regulations
2. Overall vision and goals of executive leadership. At this point, these may simply be the goals you wish to see adopted by the leadership.
3. Listing of all direct and indirect stakeholders, with points of contact
4. Listing of technical experts who can help evaluate current systems, outline specifications for improvements and identify backup requirements.
5. Current situation, including strengths, weaknesses, opportunities and threats
6. Desired outcome in specific operational terms from the perspective of key stakeholders
7. Desired timetable
8. Identification of known or anticipated obstacles
9. Outline of position statements for any constituencies that may be opposed to action.
10. Flow chart of the decision-making process, including who will need to review, approve and fund the proposal

The successful planning effort will be a dynamic balance between mission support goals, technical considerations, stakeholder politics and budget realities.

It is often helpful to have planning meetings chaired or moderated by a skilled team facilitator, even if that individual has no specific background in communications. Colleges, agency trainers and social service departments are often excellent sources for people with meeting facilitation skills.

Credibility of the planning process is maintained when every stakeholder knows they are free to speak candidly, offer dissenting views, and advocate unpopular positions.

The aim of the process should be to attain consensus, the point at which every stakeholder is able to say without hesitation, "The agency I represent can support this decision."

Advance planning is essential if any disaster response is to be successful, and this is particularly true when highly technical issues must be resolved in the context of multiple agency priorities, competing stakeholders, diverse constituencies and budget constraints. Unfortunately, unplanned emergency communications are often set up immediately following a disaster where they complicate the situation, rather than bringing the immediate help that was intended. Just a few of the complications regularly experienced with hastily installed emergency communications systems are:

- Temporary emergency systems can interfere with existing parts of the fixed system.
- Temporary systems may not fill the most critical gaps.
- Operators of the temporary system may not be fully trusted by response authorities needing support.
- Temporary systems may not efficiently interface with existing infrastructure and decision-support systems.
- Temporary systems may be prohibitively costly.
- Temporary systems, installers and operators may not be obtainable in a widespread catastrophic event.

There must be a clear understanding of the strengths, weaknesses, opportunities and threats of both the existing system and temporary solutions before any disaster response and recovery strategy is considered.

A comprehensive planning effort must begin with two fundamental questions before it is possible to determine what is needed, either as system improvements or as contingency backup:

1. What are the critical communications needs of our community? (Referred to as a Baseline Needs Assessment)

2. What systems do we now have, how do they work, and what are their vulnerabilities?

The following sections outline an information-gathering and assessment approach that should aid most planning efforts, whether planning for a new system, developing upgrades to an existing system, or mobilizing disaster emergency contingency resources.

Planning Challenges

The following challenges are often cited* as obstacles to effective planning:

1. Many organizations do not consider communications planning to be a priority and do not allocate sufficient resources to it.
2. Communications planning efforts often do not include all stakeholders.
3. Personnel responsible for designing or procuring communications systems are sometimes unaware of the status of communications standards.
4. The number and diversity of emergency response agencies adds to the complexity and difficulty of finding solutions that meet the needs of all users.
5. Standards development is hindered by the diverse requirements of independent emergency response organizations and agencies.
6. Communications interoperability across national, state, local , tribal, private-sector and international systems are often hindered by the use of encryption by one or more parties that cannot or is not shared.
7. There is insufficient information about testing and assessing emergency response systems, which makes it difficult for emergency response agencies to make informed procurement decisions about technology applications. The challenge is even more serious for long-term planning and budget projection.
8. State and local government agencies do not consistently participate in standards-making bodies and development process.
9. A common view of existing incident conditions and resources is not readily available or easily shared among federal, state, tribal and local jurisdictions in a way that improves the understanding of the emergency or event. The private sector and international bodies have even more difficulty obtaining a clear view.
10. Despite the proliferation of "standards," the marketplace is filled with competing proprietary technologies that make rational systems decisions exceedingly difficult.

The challenges are getting more difficult, not easier.

The only approach with any hope of success is comprehensive planning, effective systems analysis, and thorough contingency preparedness, as outlined in the following pages.

---

*As an example, refer to the section on national standards and emerging technologies.in the *National Emergency Communications Plan*, published by the U.S. Department of Homeland Security,

Basic Considerations

In designing any system, it is important to be as specific as possible when detailing the qualities and features that are needed. Later in this section there will be discussions of *Current Systems Assessment* and *Baseline Needs Assessment*; however, in order to establish a foundation for those assessments, we should first define the qualities and features that will come into play.

You may find that you want to add to the following list of features normally associated with communications systems:

Term	Meaning
Capability	Capability refers to a clear statement of what a system is able to do. For example, "Provide one half-duplex analog voice channel from county dispatch center to mobile units throughout Washington County, with 95% coverage of all areas in the county."
Reliability	Reliability is best expressed as a percentage of time the system must be fully functioning. When it is not practical to specify a percentage, relative terms such as *Very High,* or *High* can be used as general descriptions.
Flexibility	Flexibility refers to the ability of a system to adapt to circumstances different from normal operations. For example, can operations be changed simply by the user throwing a switch or must the entire system be taken offline so that technicians can make modifications.
Usability	Usability refers to how easy the system is to use and its "friendliness" towards users, as well as whether it actually performs the job it is intended to do without excessive difficulty.
Deliverability	Deliverability asks whether the system as designed can actually be put into service.
Maintainability	Maintainability refers to the ease with which systems can be kept operational and reliable. Logistics issues such as access to equipment, availability of skilled technicians with replacement parts and test equipment are all part of the maintainability equation.
Security	System security has many components: Physical security and defensibility of hardware; vulnerability of the system to cyber attack; ability to use encryption or other methods to keep information from falling into the wrong hands; ability to confirm the authenticity of messages; and positive identification of senders and receivers.

Interoperability	Interoperability refers to the ability to easily exchange messages among all those needing to do so. In practice, the term usually refers to the ability of on-scene responders from different agencies to talk with one another over radios, regardless of manufacturer.
Restorability	Restorability considers the speed and cost of repairing a damaged system and returning it to its pre-damaged capabilities.
Life-Cycle Affordability	Life-Cycle Affordability refers to the total cost of building, maintaining and disposing of a system from its installation through eventual replacement, in relation to available funding sources throughout the entire period. This is one of the most frequently overlooked aspects of communications system planning.

Both in assessing current systems and planning improvements, it may be helpful to rate every alternative in terms of each of these features. For less complex systems, general terms such as "High, Medium or Low" may be sufficiently descriptive for each feature. In highly complex systems, it may be helpful to assign numerical rankings to each feature.

It may also be helpful to rank-order the features in your study, so that the most critical features are highlighted.

Baseline Needs Assessment

While this is presented as the "first step" in communications planning, in reality, needs assessment will be an ongoing process throughout the entire planning process, but it is the essential starting point.

Developing a baseline needs assessment is a lot like "Zero Based Budgeting," where the aim is to wipe the slate clean and start from the very beginning to identify and prioritize needs. Done properly, this process helps to identify true needs while breaking free of preconceived notions and the momentum of current operations. The challenge, of course, is in getting agency representatives to actually go back to the basics and identify true requirements, rather than just assume that they need to build on past practices.

The Baseline Needs Assessment consists of identifying:

1. Critical missions
2. Essential support activities
3. Vital communications* needs

*For simplicity, this section uses the term *communications* to refer to all forms of information exchange, message processing and decision-support. The degree to which your planning effort extends into information technology, data processing, decision making, command-control authority, computer-aided support and related fields is dependent on individual circumstances and your planning resources, but the more comprehensive your study, the better the final results.

Critical Missions

The first planning step is to identify the critical missions of your organization.

Critical missions can generally be defined as those activities that are so important to your organization that failure to attain your intended objectives in these key areas will have unacceptable consequences.

Critical missions are those undertakings that give your organization its purpose for being. Often, they are stated in the organization's charter, and for governmental entities they are almost always detailed in laws, regulations and orders.

It is possible that circumstances so overwhelm an organization that all critical missions cannot be accomplished at the same time. For instance, if a fire department defines its mission as to "save lives and protect property," and a situation develops where resources do not allow the department to do both, is it clear which mission takes priority? Does the higher priority mission take all resources away from the lower one, or just some resources?

While the above fire department example might have an obvious answer, the issue of critical mission priority can become very contentious during actual emergencies. Does the public works department clear debris from the road leading to the hospital or put all its resources into building temporary protective levees around public buildings? What gets priority, fuel for the water treatment plant or fuel for generators at radio repeater sites?

Only through a clear consensus regarding an organization's list of critical missions is it even possible to proceed with communications planning to support those missions.

It is possible that there will be differences of opinion among an organization's leadership regarding which missions are truly critical and which are simply very important. The communications planning process may indeed help leadership resolve—or at least identify-- these differences in understanding before a crisis develops.

Completing a table similar to the following should be helpful in clearly identifying an organization's most critical missions:

Critical Missions Worksheet

Mission	Priority	Required by	Typical Activity	Failure Impact

As an example, the following critical missions might be identified by a local government:

Critical Missions – City of Bryson

Mission	Priority	Required by	Typical Activity	Failure Impact
Search and Rescue		State Law 45-3 Ordnance 1	SAR teams deploy, supported by EMS, Police, city mutual aid	Death or serious injury
Emergency Medicine		State Law 45-3 Ordnance 2	EMS district sends ALS unit to scene.	Death or serious injury
Fire Fighting		State Law 45-3 Ordnance 2	FD crews & equipment go to scene	Death, serious injury, large property loss
Public Alert & Warning		State Law 138-99 Ordnance 8	Activate outdoor sirens. Radio, TV, cable alerts	Death, injury, uninformed public
Law Enforcement		State Law 45-3 Ordnance 2	Emergency response. Patrols.	Death, injury, crime, vigilantes
Evacuation		State Law 47-15 Ordnance 8	Traffic control. Issue public instructions	Death, injury, public confusion
Sheltering		State Law 47-15 Ordnance 26	Open shelters, inform public	Health & safety risk.
Debris Removal		Town Charter Ordnance 196	Public Works crews & equip. open roads	Traffic disruption Delayed emerg.
Utilities & Sanitation		Town Charter Ordnance 486	Restore power, water sewer	Risk to public health & commerce

The following critical missions are often cited by governmental agencies:

- Command and Control
- Alert and Warning
- Fire Fighting
- Law Enforcement
- Search and Rescue
- Emergency Medical Services
- Public Health and Hospitals
- Evacuation
- Mass Care: Feeding and Sheltering
- Public Utilities
- Debris Removal
- Public Information and Accountability
- Continuity of Government Operations
- Continuity of Commerce
- Infrastructure Protection and Restoration

The following critical missions are often cited by nongovernmental and volunteer organizations:

- Team Coordination and Control
- Public Information
- Mass Care: Water, Feeding and Sheltering
- Logistics
- Emergency Medical Care
- Public Health and Sanitation
- Special Needs Support
- Staff Feeding, Sheltering, Security
- Communications with staff in the field
- Staff Evacuation

After identification of your organization's critical missions, the next step is to identify the essential support activities needed to ensure the success of those missions.

Essential Support Activities

For each critical mission, it is likely that there will be several essential support activities that an organization must undertake in order to make the mission a success. For example, response vehicles need to be refueled, crews need to be fed and housed, and the public needs to be kept informed. In most cases, support activities involve a wide range of agencies whose work—when it's done successfully—is nearly invisible to everyone except those directly involved.

It is very easy to overlook these invisible but essential support activities when focusing on the communications plan. Often the supporting activities use separate radio nets and command-control structures and it's just assumed that they will take care of themselves. The comprehensive communications plan will include systems needed by support activities, even if only included as an annex to the basic plan.

A good planning strategy is to develop a separate table for each of the Critical Mission line items (see page 21), that the essential support activities needed by that critical mission. If, for example, your organization identifies four critical missions, you would then develop four separate Essential Support Activity tables, one for each of the critical missions

Essential Support Activity Worksheet
For Critical Mission _____

Support Activity	Priority	Provided by	Typical Activity	Failure Impact

While the worksheets for Critical Missions and Essential Support Activities will probably continue to be revised throughout the planning process, attaining consensus on an initial draft represents an important milestone in the planning process. With basic agreement on what is critical and essential, your organization will be in a good position to start planning the critical communications infrastructure that is absolutely necessary for mission success, followed by an assessment of options for backup systems needed to reduce the risk of critical systems failure.

At this point in the planning process, it will be helpful to include subject matter experts with knowledge about current and emerging communications technologies, if that has not already been done. As planning progresses from this point on, the amount of technical detail required will necessarily increase, as will the importance of making informed choices regarding systems design.

Critical Mission Communications Requirements

While this inquiry starts with the question "Who needs to talk with whom?" there will be many questions to follow, including:

- What kind of information needs to be communicated?

- In what form is that information best communicated?

- How quickly does it need to be delivered?

- Do delivery and understanding need to be acknowledged?

- What is the optimal route for sending that information?

- Does anyone else need to know?

- Does the information need to be protected or kept confidential?

- Do sender and receiver need to authenticate their identities?

- What is the mission impact if information does not get delivered or if it is misinterpreted?

- What is the mission impact if the information is compromised or accessed by unauthorized parties?

Communications Requirements
For Critical Mission _____

Between Whom	Urgency	Format / Mode	Security / Accuracy	Failure Impact

Assessing the Current System

Most communications systems are the result of many decades of evolution, compromise and patchwork modification. As a result, the system may operate with less than ideal efficiency and be weakened with critical vulnerabilities, some known and others still to be discovered.

The very first step in disaster communications planning is to accomplish a thorough and candid assessment of your systems as they now exist.

It is generally not enough just to catalog details about the radio network itself, although the radio system usually is a critical consideration. A thorough assessment of how information flows into and out of decision-making centers is essential. The very best approach would be to catalog then analyze every communications channel and decision support mechanism required to provide public safety. Clearly this requires a massive effort for all but the simplest of settings, therefore total and complete cataloging may not be practical. However, identification, cataloging and circuit analysis of the very most critical channels is essential.

It's also not enough just to look at the systems under your control, but to consider how other systems interconnect with yours. For example, what critical information do you receive or send over the public telephone network, commercial paging systems, or radio/TV broadcast stations, and what would be the impact on your operation if those services were disrupted or degraded?

As one illustration, consider how a fully functioning Public Service Answering Point (PSAP or 911 Center) would be affected if a community's entire telephone system went down because of a fire in the telephone company's central office (switching center). How would the public report emergencies? How would public agencies send information back to the public? Do the remote control, voice and data circuits for public safety radio networks, paging systems, and mobile data terminals go through that central office? These questions ought to be just as important to emergency managers as the question of dispatch system design and radio systems architecture, as the answers to these questions should provide insights into ways public safety communications systems can be designed and backed up for maximum reliability.

One helpful approach is to diagram the complete process by which a member of the public reports a fire, a call-taker assesses, categorizes and routes that call, a dispatcher sends firefighters and other responders, the incident commander communicates with the response team and requests additional resources, and how a multiagency response, if needed, gets coordinated.

Focus should be on overall communications linkages, decision aids and potential single points of failure.

Your diagram for each of the critical communications flows might look something like the flow chart on the next page and your catalog might look like the spreadsheet that follows. In a highly complex system, it might be necessary to catalog hundreds, if not thousands, of unique information flows. If planning time and resources are limited, you would, of course, focus on the most critical linkages first, but keep in mind that it is important to fully account for public communications and interface with other agencies even in very small systems.

The more specific your communications diagrams and subsystems catalogs, the more accurate will be your overall analysis. Remember, at this point the purpose is to collect information about how systems operate and interconnect as well as to identify vulnerabilities and the impact of failures. While it is tempting to start creating solutions as you go along, it would be premature to do so before a complete systems analysis is accomplished.

As a minimum, the baseline planning survey should include:

- Responsible parties for each branch of the system
- Critical switching centers for the public telephone network
- Call routing and switching systems for your internal telephone network
- Critical data support systems
- Routing of voice, data and control signals from command/dispatch centers to radio transmitter and receiver sites, whether by wireline, cable, microwave or other technology
- Location and security of radio base stations, remote units, repeaters and relay points
- Identification and interoperability specifics for all users of the system
- Primary and backup electrical power resources for all critical components of the system
- Modes of potential failure at each critical system component, with particular emphasis on single points of failure that can disrupt the entire system.
- Failure indicators: How can symptoms that warn of impending failure be used to trigger alarms?

Communications Flow Analysis

Start with what you already know about the critical communications systems you will be researching. At this point, it will not be worth the investment of time and energy to produce fancy charts because you will be adding to and changing the flow diagrams as you obtain additional information about the systems.

It may be helpful for planning teams to use electronic whiteboards or computer tablets to initially sketch communications flow diagrams, particularly if copies of the diagrams can be stored and shared. Even if the diagram is just quickly sketched on plain paper, it can be scanned and shared.

Your end result might look something like the following, but right after this example, there will be a step-by-step guide for gathering the information you need and displaying it in a useful form.

Sample Communications Flow Diagram

Make a separate sketch for each major branch of the overall system.

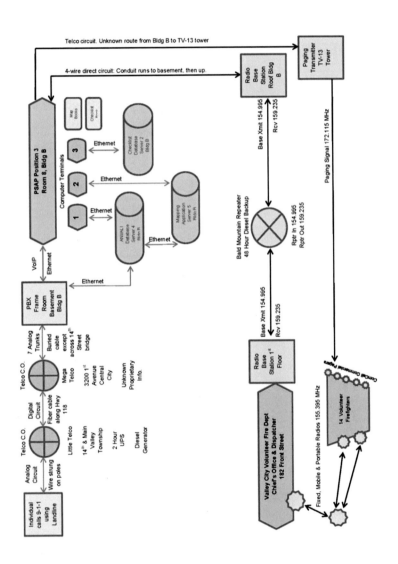

Sample Communications System Catalog

Washington County PSAP – Bryson City Rural Areas North & West of Valley Township Subsystem Catalog for Public Calls & Fire Dispatch					
Component Subsystem	Location	Responsible Agency	Contact	Key Vulnerability & Impact	Notes
Rural Telephone Cables	Rural Areas North & West of Valley Township	Little Telephone Company, Inc.	Fred Jones 555-555-1997	Cable breakage. Loss of all POTS service north & west of Valley Township	70 year old cables. Damaged, leaning poles. Trees overgrown. (Estimated that only 4 households have alternative phone service)
Cellular Service	Rural Areas North & West of Valley Township	Varzine Wireless, Inc.	National Network Center 800-555-1200	Unprotected T-1 pedestal beside road. UPS only, no generator. Loss of all cell service to Valley Township & rural areas	Cell antennas located on abandoned grain elevator Poor coverage North & West.
Valley Township Central Office	14th & Main Valley Township	Little Telephone Company, Inc.	Fred Jones 555-555-1997	Unprotected flood zone. Loss of all POTS service in Valley Township & rural areas	Switch on 1st floor. Water system fire sprinklers. 2 Hour UPS. Diesel generator and 50 gallon tank.
Bryson City Central Office	3200 1st Avenue Bryson City	MegaTelco, International	Regional Network Center 800-555-1000	Unknown vulnerability. Loss of all POTS service in Bryson City and long distance service for entire state.	Local Carrier Central Office and AP&P Tandem Switch in one building. MegaTelco will not release proprietary info. 10% households use alternate phone service.

Telephone Cables to County Building	From 3200 1st Ave to Courthouse Bldg "B" Bryson City	MegaTelco International	Regional Network Center 800-555-1000	Ice jams can cut cable under 14th Street Bridge. Loss of all POTS to County Building	Cables poorly maintained and hanging low over water. County has limited outgoing backup via VoIP (RomCast Cable Service)
County Building Private Branch Exchange	Basement County Bldg "B" Bryson City	County IT Department	Joe Smith, Director of IT 555-555-6666	Fire damage or loss of electricity. Loss of all telephones and data in County Buildings	Adjacent to boiler room. 2 Hour UPS and 65 year old diesel generator. Cables are 1984 ethernet run through PVC conduit…not in compliance with present wiring code.
ANI/ALI Database Server	4th Floor County Bldg "B" Bryson City	County IT Department. Data provided by LotharSys (dynamic update)	Joe Smith, Director of IT 555-555-6666	Loss of electricity. No location information displayed to dispatchers	Server #4 in County IT Center. Warm backup 5 min to 1 hour switchover. 2 hour UPS. 65 year old diesel generator.
Dispatch Mapping Application	4th Floor County Bldg "B" Bryson City	County IT Department. Data provided by MapsR-Us (on-call update)	Joe Smith, Director of IT 555-555-6666	Loss of electricity. No mapping information displayed to dispatchers	Server #5 in County IT Center. Warm backup 5 min to 1 hour switchover. 2 hour UPS. 65 year old diesel generator. System fails frequently due to software glitches. Backup is map book.

Dispatch Checklist Application	4th Floor County Bldg "B" Bryson City	County IT Department.	Joe Smith, Director of IT 555-555-6666	Loss of electricity. No call-taker response checklist information displayed to dispatchers	Server #2 in County IT Center. Warm backup 5 min to 1 hour switchover. 2 hour UPS. 65 year old diesel generator.
County Fire Radio Dispatch Base Station	Roof (Elevator Penthouse) County Bldg "B" Bryson City	County Sheriff	Ron's Real Reliable Radio 555-555-9876	Lightning strike or loss of electricity. Inability to talk with fire stations or incident commanders	10 year old Motorachi VHF radio base station. Must relay through Bald Mountain Repeater to the west or Bryson City water tank repeater to the east. Range limited to 15 miles without repeaters. Mobiles must know to switch to channel "2" if repeaters fail.
Bald Mountain Fire Radio Repeater	Bald Mountain County Park. Small metal shelter & 25' tower at top of dirt road.	County Sheriff	Ron's Real Reliable Radio 555-555-9876	Lightning strike, vandalism or loss of electricity. Inability to talk with fire stations or incident commanders	10 year old Motorachi repeater. Frequent vandalism. No UPS but 48 hour propane generator backup.
County Fire Paging System	TV-13 tower 7 miles north of Bryson City	Cabs-n-Mor Paging Service, Inc.	Rob Roberts 555-555-1389	Unknown. Loss of ability to page-out firefighters from all departments in the county	Link to paging transmitter uses phone lines. Vendor will not give specifics of system at TV-13 tower.
Valley Twp Volunteer Fire Dept Radio Base Station	182 Front St. Valley Township	Fire Chief Valley Township VFD	Chief Burton 555-555-2929	Lightning strike or loss of electricity. Inability to talk with	New Hendix M-5 radio, old antenna. Can switch to two

				dispatch or incident commanders	alternate channels.
Valley Twp Volunteer Fire Dept Mobiles	182 Front St. Valley Township	Fire Chief Valley Township VFD	Chief Burton 555-555-2929	Site visit scheduled January 18th	New Hendix M-9000 mobile radios: One in Chief's SUV, one in Engine 6, one in Pumper 9, one in Wildland 4, one in Tender 3. Can switch to two alternate channels.
Valley Twp Volunteer Fire Dept Portables	182 Front St. Valley Township	Fire Chief Valley Township VFD	Chief Burton 555-555-2929	Site visit scheduled January 18th	New Hendix H-300 portable radios. Chief, two deputy chiefs, four volunteer captains and six volunteer lieutenants keep radios full time. 12 additional radios available to distribute on-scene. All can switch to two alternate channels.
ARES Auxiliary Emergency Communications	Various	ARES District Emergency Coordinator	Joe Finch WX5XMA 555-555-3864	Meeting scheduled February 4th	22 registered volunteers in county. 14 mobile or portable units, 8 with SUV & 4 with snowmobiles 2 with boats; 9 with high power HF units, 14 with VHF voice and data systems

The above communications flow diagram and communications subsystem catalogue illustrate the degree of detail necessary to accomplish a comprehensive systems analysis. Your particular system may require more or less detail, but these examples should provide a good start for most planning efforts.

Why so much detail? Why not just get on with designing a new system?

Without complete knowledge and understanding of the *entire* communications, information processing and decision-making systems, any changes can hardly be more than tinkering. Without profound knowledge of those systems in the context of their environment, any form of change or contingency planning is little more than taking a gamble and hoping you're lucky.

The following examples are intended to provide background for the kinds of questions needed for the systems surveys, catalogues and communications flow diagrams a comprehensive planning effort will need.

If you were making the initial sketch of the system shown on page 30, the first diagram might look something like this:

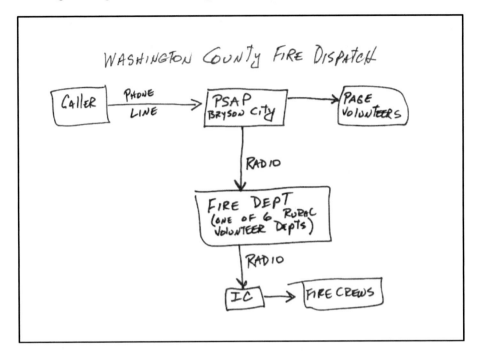

Using this as a starting point, the planning team would begin asking questions about different parts of the system for which additional information will be needed. It will be helpful to record questions as they arise, for sometimes even the simplest of questions, such as "How does a phone call actually get from a house in Valley Township to the Public Service Answering Point (PSAP) in Bryson City?" may eventually lead to discovery of significant information.

Initial questions and comments from the planning team might be recorded as follows:

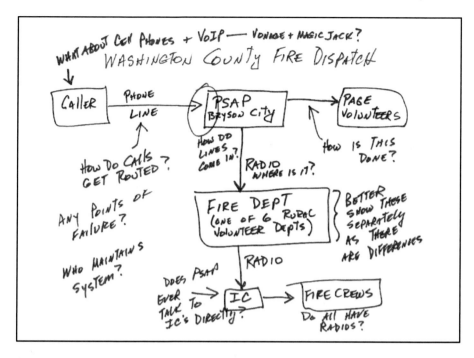

As you can see, starting with even the simplest of sketches, the communications flow diagram can start to structure the planning team's thinking about how processes work, where vulnerabilities might be and—most importantly—the parts of the system about which little is known. By following up on these questions and others that followed, the planning team was able to draft the reasonably complete diagram on page 16 as backed up by more detailed information on the systems catalog. Ideally, even the finished diagram on page 16 would be subject to continued refinement as more technical detail is learned about the system.

It is best to have both system users and members of the technical staff represented on the planning team and cooperating to develop the diagrams. Users know how the flow of communications actually works and the technical staff will know...or can find out...how things are wired together.

The more detailed the communications flow diagrams, the better will be your understanding of how the system works and where the critical points of failure are likely to be found. The planning teams that ask the most "How?" and "Why?" questions are most likely to succeed.

The following sketch includes additional information the planning team has discovered, as well as some new questions regarding actual operation of the system:

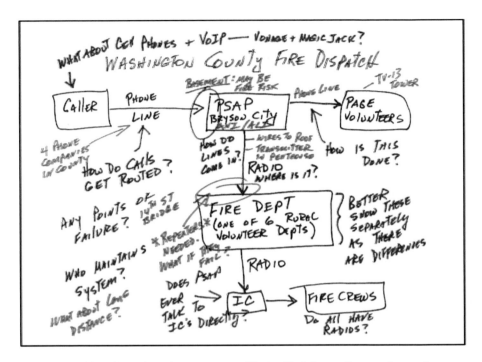

Once a working flow chart becomes so filled with information and questions that it becomes difficult to read, it is time to redraw it or move the detail and questions to a separate document, such as the communications system catalog on page 17. The advantage of continuing to use the flow chart, even when the system is relatively well defined, is that flow charts help to focus discussions while allowing the planning team to visualize the relationship that subsystems have to one another.

Key questions that the team should investigate are:

- Who initiates messages, calls, reports or transmissions?
- What method do they use?
- Through what media are the messages/calls routed?
- What is the physical routing?
- Where are the switching or routing points?
- At what point do messages get routed from one subsystem to another?
- What agency is responsible for operating and maintaining the individual subsystem?
- What are the likely points of failure?

A comprehensive study will incorporate not only primary communications systems, but backup, auxiliary and emergency systems as well.

Primary Communications Systems

Primary communications systems, as their name implies, are the main systems an organization uses every day.

The chart on the following page can be used to catalog details about these systems.

Primary Communications Systems

System Name	Used By	Maintained By	Backed Up By	Description

Backup Communications Systems

Backup communications systems are defined as capabilities that can be very rapidly activated. For example, if a radio channel fails for any reason, a backup channel can be accessed by operators making a manual switch or the system sensing a fault and switching automatically. To accomplish this without delay or disruption requires advance planning, training, and system tests.

Backup systems should be documented and tracked just like primary systems.

Backup Communications Systems

System Name	Backs Up	Maintained By	Time to Activate	Description

Auxiliary Communications Systems

Auxiliary communications systems can be described as preplanned systems kept in ready reserve. Often, auxiliary equipment and operators need to be brought in from the outside, and the time needed to mobilize these resources may result in temporary disruption of service. Frequently, auxiliary capability is considerably different from primary and backup services; those relying on the auxiliary capability need to be trained in the differences.

Auxiliary communications can range from teams of Amateur Radio Emergency Service® (ARES) volunteers to support from contractors.

For planning purposes, *auxiliary communications* should be defined as on-call resources within the authority and jurisdiction of the primary systems manager. For example, if the jurisdiction's emergency management office has an agreement with a local ARES team and has included ARES in the contingency response plan, then ARES can be considered an auxiliary communications asset. The same would be true of reserve police or fire communications teams or on-call contractors.

In general, auxiliary systems should be separate from primary and backup systems, so that no credible failure scenario is likely to completely disrupt all three.

The following worksheet can be used to identify preplanned auxiliary support and will highlight areas where additional critical support may be needed.

Auxiliary Communications Systems

Auxiliary System Name	Supports	Provided By	Time to Activate	Description

Emergency Communications Systems

Documentation is needed for any preplanned emergency communications support that will be sent in from the outside during an emergency.

Examples might include mobilization of National Guard resources, activation of mutual aid agreements, cross-border support such as the Emergency Management Assistance Compact (EMAC), federal assistance from FEMA or the Department of Defense.

It is important not to make *assumptions* about outside support. Document only those systems for which there is a Memorandum of Agreement, finalized plan, contract or other solid indicator assuring the availability of emergency support.

Later in the planning process we will undertake a Gap Analysis to identify unmet emergency communications needs.

You may use the following worksheet to document preplanned emergency communications support:

Preplanned Emergency Communications Systems

Emergency System Name	Supports	Provided By	Time to Activate	Description & Controlling Document

Hazard and Threat Identification

The next step in the process is to identify specific hazards and threats that might threaten your critical communications systems.

Hazards are those elements in the operational environment that can potentially cause harm if not eliminated, mitigated or taken into account.

Hazards caused by people are often referred to as "threats,"

Examples of hazards include lightning, flash floods, landslides and other adverse environmental factors. Threats may include sabotage, faulty maintenance, and systems degradation due to neglect, or the reality (not just potential) of an impending, certain flood.

For simplicity, the following planning process combines hazards and threats into a single consideration, although technically there is a distinction between the two when conducting a sophisticated, high-level analysis.

While every system is different, most systems will have some degree of vulnerability to the following hazards and threats:

- Facility emergency, such as fire or evacuation
- Environmental impact, such as lightning, flood, or weather extremes
- Malevolent damage, such as from sabotage or theft
- Maintenance mishap
- Degradation due to neglect or lack of maintenance resources
- Obsolescence

You will likely identify many additional risks to your system, based on a careful review of past events and a thorough assessment of your operations environment.

The following questions should help to identify hazards and threats:

1. During the past 100 years, what events have caused destruction or disruption in the geographical area served by the communications system? (Examples: Tornado, flood, wildfire, hurricane, earthquake.)
2. During the lifetime of the existing communications system, what failures occurred and what caused them?
3. What new threats or hazards are emerging in your area? (For example, changing weather patterns, changed land use, new dams or other new activity that changes the environment.)
4. What technical hazards or threats do your system operators believe are credible? (Examples, power failure or cyberattack.)

5. What events have caused failures or disruption for other agencies operating systems similar to yours?
6. What adverse events have affected neighboring communities?

Credible Threat Identification

As outlined in the previous section, hazards and threats are events such as fire, flood, transportation disruption, criminal activity, violence in the workplace, civil disorder, severe weather, and everything else that can harm you and your systems. For simplicity, we will just refer to both kinds of events as "threats."

Credible threats are those that you believe have some likelihood of actually happening.

Some organizations use the one-chance-in-a-hundred-per-year rule of thumb to determine what a credible threat is. The actual definition will depend on your community, your organization and your tolerance for uncertainty.

There are various approaches you may wish to take in identifying credible threats. The following resources may be able to assist:

- The state emergency management office
- Local emergency managers
- Fire departments and law enforcement agencies
- Research or reference desk at the local library
- Research and statistics departments of colleges and universities
- Climatic and weather records
- Long-time residents of the community
- Experienced members within your organization

After listing all the hazards and threats you can identify, develop focus for the list by estimating the likelihood that such an event would happen in any given year. Keep in mind that as climate changes and weather patterns shift, what was once considered a "Thousand Year Flood" with an annual probability of 0.001 may now be a "Hundred Year Flood" with an annual probability of 0.01 or a "Ten Year Flood" with an annual probability of 0.1.

College and University statistics departments can help with this assessment, but in the end there will be a lot of educated guessing.

System Impact Analysis

One credible threats have been identified, it will be beneficial to explore the various ways a given event would likely affect your systems. Many threats will impact diverse parts of systems differently, and sometimes indirectly.

As an example, a flood may have no immediate impact on mountaintop repeaters, but may wash out communications lines, fiber optic cables, or electric power lines going to the repeater. If, for instance, a flood washes out the power line, there may still be no immediate impact, because the repeater's uninterruptable power supply (UPS) and generators pick up the load. Unless the repeater has a signaling system back to your control center, there may be no indication that it is running on a limited supply of fuel for the emergency generator.

That same flood, however, may also have a secondary impact on the repeater if, for instance, the access road is washed out or impassible, and it is not possible to deliver replenishment fuel to the site. When the emergency generator's tank runs empty, the repeater will shut down. These secondary impacts of threats can be just as devastating to your system as the more immediate, primary effects.

Reviewing reports from past incidents will be helpful, as will looking at experiences of other communities during their emergencies.

Synergistic Impact Analysis

A Synergistic Impact Analysis looks at the way events can combine to compound the complexity of the impact.

For instance, a prolonged power outage may cause systems to use emergency generators which consume fuel. The outage will likely increase the demand for refueling services, at a time when fuel depots have reduced pumping capability due to the power outage. If traffic lights are also not working, it will take much longer for fuel trucks to make deliveries, and their schedules will be less predictable.

At the same time, repair technicians will be delayed in transit and may have delays in finding fuel for their service vehicles.

In completing your final assessment of the impact of each situation, it will be helpful to brainstorm the extended consequences of each credible threat.

Overall Risk Assessment

Once you are satisfied that you understand enough about hazards and threats, the next step will be to assess the actual risk, or potential impact on your systems..

One way to understand the term "risk" is this analogy: If the threat is a flood, one risk is drowning. The risk is very high if you are actually in the water. The risk is very low if you are looking at the flood from a hill top.

Risk assessment, therefore, is the process of considering the degree to which each threat has the potential of impacting parts of your system. Ris can be increased or decreased by your actions. Some dramatic events may have very little probability of harming your systems, while other seemingly innocuous events may completely disable critical processes.

Only through a careful assessment of each threat and the related risk to your systems is it possible to reach a full understanding of your vulnerabilities.

This insight should help you in prioritizing your mitigation and preparedness efforts. Clearly, you will want to emphasize threat mitigation and risk reduction to protect your most critical systems and assets.

A chart similar to the following may be helpful in this process.

Risk Assessment for Critical Systems

Threat or Hazard	System Affected	Risk	Impact	Impact Severity
100 Year flood on Main Street	Main Street Power Substation	Fire, Explosion., Site Failure	City-wide power failure	Extreme

Vulnerability Analysis

Once you have obtained a full understanding of the risks and impacts to your systems, next step in the process is to complete a system-wide vulnerability analysis, which takes the risk assessment worksheet and determines the real-world vulnerability of each system.

This analysis takes into account all mitigating and aggravating factors and your preparedness efforts, and results in a clear picture of your most likely points of failure and resulting impacts.

Continuing the example of the Main Street flood from the last section, if sandbagging could adequately protect the power substation from the flood, then the vulnerability is lessened as long as there is time to implement mitigation or protection.

Similarly, if I were possible to shut down and isolate the substation and re-route power to critical facilities from other substations, the vulnerability is lessened, although the threat and risks remain.

The vulnerability analysis should help identify those absolutely essential mitigation efforts you need to put at the top of your list, as well as reveal any remaining vulnerabilities that are either beyond your ability to control, or which must be planned for using backup systems, because you anticipate that they have a high risk of failure during the event.

The vulnerability analysis should result in a document that devotes a paragraph or chapter, depending on complexity, to each of your critical systems, and a plain-language statement of its vulnerability to failure from the most credible threats.

For example, "The main street power station is highly vulnerable to catastrophic failure in the event of a 100-Year flood on Main Street. Failure of the substation will result in loss of commercial power to all locations within the township. Risk can be reduced by a sandbag dike at least one meter high."

Gap Analysis

Simply stated, a gap analysis is a careful consideration of the gap between what you have and what you need. Gap Analysis will help identify your highest priorities for strategic improvements in the long term and contingency support should an emergency develop before your improvements are implemented.

Gap analysis can be complex, with highly refined measurements, or it can be a straight-forward, practical assessment.

If you have not already done so, conducting a capability needs assessment is needed in order to provide information for the gap analysis.

Capability Needs Assessment

The capability needs assessment asks these questions:

1. What capabilities do we need that we do not have?
2. What improvements in existing capabilities do we need?

The review uses the systems planning documents from previous pages in this book as a baseline, but goes the extra step of asking "is this good enough?"

It is usually not sufficient to base the capability needs assessment on a community's current needs, but rather the anticipated needs of the future. A five to ten year planning window is usually recommended as a minimum.

Using a template similar to the following should be sufficient to get the process started:

Needs vs Existing Capability			
DESIRED STATE	CURRENT STATE	DEFICIENCY	ACTION REQUIRED

Strategic Planning

Strategic planning goes a few steps beyond systems improvement and critical needs assessment, and looks at future environments, anticipated developments, and opportunities.

In fact, one popular approach is to use the SWOT Tool – Evaluation of Strengths / Weaknesses / Opportunities / Threats – to identify strategies that will position the organization favorably in future situations.

Strategic communications planning is beyond the scope of this book, however, there are many advantages to developing a strategic plan in addition to contingency planning, or at least using the information gathered in contingency planning as a starting point for long-term strategic planning.

In the U.S., the U.S. Department of Homeland Security through the Office of Emergency Communications sponsors a range of initiatives to assist states in strategic communications planning, and some of these resources may be available for states to use in assisting local jurisdictions.

Target Capability List

By clearly stating the capabilities eventually desired, the strategic plan can begin to address costs and methods for attaining the goal. The term generally used for this listing is the Target Capability List.

"Technology... is a queer thing. It brings you great gifts with one hand, and it stabs you in the back with the other."

~C.P. Snow, New York Times, 15 March 1971

National Interoperability Goal

Interoperability is not necessarily needed for every communications system; however the capability to be flexible and link with other systems when needed would likely benefit every single organization.

Interoperability involves many factors in addition to equipment standards-- Operating protocols, transmission media, language, and agency policies to name just a few. The U.S. Department of Homeland Security uses the chart displayed on the following page to portray the status of several factors affecting interoperability:

The national goal is to provide full interoperability among all activities needing exchange of information. That does not mean, however, that every radio can or should talk to every other radio.

Homeland Security

Interoperability Continuum

(S@FECOM

Governance	Individual Agencies Working Independently	Informal Coordination Between Agencies	Key Multidiscipline Staff Collaboration on a Regular Basis	Regional Committee Working with a Statewide Interoperability Committee
Standard Operating Procedures	Individual Agency SOPs	Joint SOPs for Planned Events	Joint SOPs for Emergencies	Regional Set of Communications SOPs	National Incident Management System Integrated SOPs
Technology	Swap Radios	Gateway	Shared Channels	Proprietary Shared Systems	Standards-based Shared Systems
Training & Exercises	General Orientation on Equipment	Single Agency Tabletop Exercises for Key Field and Support Staff	Multiagency Tabletop Exercises for Key Field and Support Staff	Multiagency Full Functional Exercise Involving All Staff	Regular Comprehensive Regional Training and Exercises
Usage	Planned Events	Localized Emergency Incidents	Regional Incident Management		Daily Use Throughout Region

Interoperability Continuum

Minimal Level → Optimal Level

Interoperability Self-Assessment Notes

_____

_____

_____

_____

_____

_____

_____

_____

_____

_____

_____

_____

_____

_____

_____

_____

_____

_____

_____

_____

_____

Contingency Planning

Contingency planning should be institutionalized as part of the regular planning process. Too often, backup and auxiliary systems are poorly designed and are deployed only in time of actual crisis, when the risk of failure is the greatest.

Careful planning for layers of backup is an important part of contingency planning.

Contingency planning is as much a mindset as it is a planning step.

As outlined in the early pages of this book, in-depth study of existing and planned systems should include a comprehensive and objective assessment of vulnerabilities and impacts of failure.

Contingency planning deals with the question, "What do we do when the system fails, gets overloaded, or needs to do something it wasn't designed to do."

It is easy to assume that neighboring jurisdictions, business partners, volunteers or vendors will be available when needed. In contingency planning, all assumptions must be clearly stated, and the best attempt possible should be made to verify validity of the assumptions and the conditions under which they are true.

As an example, many organizations plan to use satellite phones as an emergency backup to landlines. The often unstated assumptions are: (1) Satellite systems will be unaffected by the event, (2) Satellite systems will have enough capacity to support us, (3) Our ground terminals will work, (4) The people we need to call will have service, and (4) We know how to reach them.

A few years ago, a major city purchased a large number of satellite phones for public safety agencies to use in emergency. Shortly afterwards, the satellite service chosen by that city became unreliable due to unexpected failure of numerous satellites. The city's contingency plans were not revised to show that the satellite phones were unreliable, and as a result, the opportunity to arrange a secondary backup was missed. In addition, key officials who would need the satellite phones in an emergency were unaware of the system failures.

Tactical Planning

Tactical planning is often considered the bridge between dealing with today's situation and the time when the long-range strategic plan can come into play.

In reality, comprehensive tactical planning is a very difficult process fraught with error if it is not begun until time of emergency.

Good tactical planning is part of contingency planning, but it may go further than simply planning for emergencies. The tactical plan can spell out day-to-day systems relationships, procedures for dealing with both common and unusual events, and outline efficiencies that may be implemented.

The tactical plan might, for instance, show a temporary link between adjacent jurisdiction's radio systems during mutual aid incidents, or a temporary disconnect of a link when there are separate, unrelated incidents.

The tactical plan should be as clear and detailed as possible, with action checklists and systems diagrams, so that managers and operators can make good decisions during emergencies.

Tactical Gap Analysis

The tactical gap analysis process does not need to be long and involved, but it needs to clearly state what critical needs are lacking for credible response scenarios that might happen with little or no advance warning.

By clearly identifying the gap between what's needed and what you have in each situation, managers will be assisted in making decisions about calling for mutual aid, assistance from higher levels of government, or contractor support.

A chart similar to the following may be helpful:

Tactical Deficiencies			
REQUIRED RESOURCE	AVAILABLE	DEFICIENCY	ACTION REQUIRED

Detailed Tactical Planning

The tactical gap analysis can evolve into a more comprehensive document that guides decisions regarding short-term procurement, mutual aid arrangements, and other support arrangements. As a minimum, however, clearly stating tactical deficiencies is vital to good decision making during any incident.

This following pages will focus on the more immediate aspects of tactical planning leading up to and during an emergency, but it is highly recommended that organizations conduct detailed tactical planning well in advance of emergency situations.

Standard Operating Procedures (SOPs)

Many organizations use standard operating procedures (SOPs) or Emergency Action Guides (EAGs) for their day-to-day activities.

Having SOPs is especially important during emergencies, when staff members are under stress or filling different roles than their normal jobs.

SOPs should address the transition from normal to emergency operations and present actions in a step-by-step.

Emergency actions related to communications often involve activation of backup systems, moving equipment, and initiation of repairs or calling for mutual aid. Without standard procedures in place, every decision will be difficult and require time and attention from managers.

Field Operations Guides

Field Operations Guides are quick reference materials provided to people working outside their normal office environment, giving them access to critical information, resources, and decision tools needed during emergencies.

Examples of these guides include frequency charts, emergency contact lists, organizational do's and don'ts, maps, and other information appropriate to the organization.

Guides are often printed on durable waterproof paper, spiral bound, and sized to fit in the pocket of a shirt, cargo pants, or the outer pouch of a back pack.

Emergency Resource Lists

The organization needs a contact list for all resources that might be needed during an emergency.

The list should be as complete as possible and include all available information about suppliers, such as:

> Primary and secondary telephone numbers
> After-hours numbers
> Names of key personnel
> Street address
> FAX Number
> Email

Someone should be responsible for a periodic verification of all information on the list. The most critical resources should be kept up to date all the time, and the complete list verified at least annually, if not more frequently.

Mutual Aid Agreements

Most organizations would benefit from having mutual aid agreements prior to an emergency.

Such agreements provide for one party to help another in time of need, provided that they are able to do so without undue impact on their own mission.

Everything from loaning of equipment and personnel to joint use of facilities can be included in agreement, as well as statements regarding reimbursement rates, liability issues, and worker's compensation arrangements.

By negotiating agreements before an emergency, each organization's legal department can carefully consider implications, and standard operating procedures (SOPs) can be developed in both organizations to incorporate mutual aid capabilities.

Self-Healing Systems

Modern systems design can include built-in self-test capabilities, and many systems are able to automatically reconfigure themselves as components fail or become degraded.

It is critically important that the systems communicate their status to human operators.

In many cases, however, the fail state is only indicated by a small indicator on a subcomponent that may not draw the attention of an operator or maintenance worker. Unless the technician is looking for indicators, the system may have activated its last available backup without anyone realizing that there is a problem.

Complete knowledge of self-healing systems is vital to reliable operation, and every effort needs to be made to ensure that systems clearly communicate their status to users or at least key operators.

Built-In Redundancy

Whenever possible, critical systems should be designed with built-in redundancy. For example, a critical radio repeater located on a remote mountaintop should have several levels of backup: The repeater itself will likely incorporate built-in self-test and be able to switch to another circuit card under some circumstances. However, if the entire repeater fails for any reason, the very best system design will provide for a backup repeater at the site to be immediately activated from the control center. If the entire repeater site fails, such as might happen during a storm or wildfire, the ideal solution would be a backup site at another location providing coverage for the most critical locations.

Such built-in redundancy is important for all critical systems.

Hot, Warm, Cold Backups

The commercial Information Technology community has honed the concept of backup sites to a science. The same concepts can apply to backups for emergency operations centers, dispatch centers, communications sites, and just about every other critical resource.

Hot backups run 24X7 as complete mirrors for the primary location. Generally the hot site has minimal staffing, but is able to take over all activities of the primary site with no warning and no loss of data. Hot sites are extremely expensive to maintain.

Warm backups generally are not staffed sufficiently to take over immediately, but they usually have a mirror of all data coming into the primary site. Sometimes, however, the data is on storage media that make time to load, and it may not be absolutely current, so it is possible there will be a gap representing lost data. Usually, all that's needed is for staff to open up the warm site and take over. As a rule, warm sites are expensive to maintain, but they are much cheaper than hot sites.

Cold sites are essentially new work stations for displaced workers, having roughly equivalent capabilities to home facilities, but without data from the primary site until someone brings it with them. Cold sites are not nearly as expensive as warm sites, but they are often the only alternative available.

An important industry rule to keep in mind: Backup sites that are kept on retainer by your organization are also retained by others. The industry rule is that the first customer declaring an emergency and providing full operational funding for the site gets possession. Others declaring disaster later, even though they have a retainer contract, must go elsewhere.

Public agencies often find it advantageous to develop mutual aid agreements with other agencies for relocation in time of emergency. By planning ahead, it is often possible to achieve a high level of emergency capability, approaching that provided by the usual Hot Site backup, at greatly reduced cost.

Auxiliary Communications Resources

Many organizations will benefit from establishing auxiliary resources for communications.

Auxiliary resources are those held in reserve that can be called up in time of emergency. Examples might be the use of roads and grounds crews to augment security during an emergency, or having environmental health technicians set up first aid stations until emergency medical teams arrive.

For communications, auxiliary teams provide exceptionally valuable capabilities, often at little or no cost to the organization.

U.S. and Canadian military organizations make extensive use of auxiliary communicators through the Military Auxiliary Radio System, the Civil Air Patrol, the Coast Guard Auxiliary, and their Canadian counterparts.

Government agencies at all levels as well as Non-Governmental Organizations (NGOs), particularly Volunteer Agencies Active in Disaster (VOADs), have access to volunteer teams from the Amateur Radio Emergency Service®, known commonly as ARES.

ARES teams can provide reliable, flexible, redundant communications, often on short notice, under the most difficult circumstances. ARES teams are generally available to participate in organizational training and exercises.

Preplanning is essential if an organization is to make use of ARES. In the U.S. and Canada, ARES is organized on a state/provincial basis, under the direction of a Section Emergency Coordinator.

More information about ARES as well as contact information for ARES emergency coordinators can be obtained from the American Radio Relay League, Newington, Connecticut, or through their website **www.arrl.org**

ARES coordinators for many states can be found by a web search for "<State Name> ARES"

There are other auxiliary communications organizations operating around the world, and any agency anticipating the need for support should make contact with the appropriate group and incorporate them into contingency planning.

Part Two: Emergency Response Guide

Managing the Unexpected

To this point, this book has aimed at assisting with comprehensive and deliberate preplanning. With good preplanning, few events will be truly unexpected. But unforeseen events do occur, and sometimes emergencies happen before you can complete your planning and preparedness process.

This section of the book is intended to help you put together a rapid tactical response, while giving you links to resources that can assist during the crisis and your transition to recovery.

Unplanned Emergency Communications

While not ideal, it is possible to assemble and manage on-the-spot emergency communications if you have a good understanding of essential system needs and have connections with resource providers.

If you are dealing with a communications emergency, the following pages are designed to provide a rapid guide to essential tasks for fast look-up of information and tips, rather than detailed explanation.

Communications Team Installing Emergency Antennas

Photo: FEMA/Bob McMillan

Systems Failure and Restoration

While the immediate task is to mobilize backup systems, restoration of the primary system is equally essential.

In most cases, the individual or company who installed the primary system is in the best position to restore it, as they will be familiar with the design, component specifications, and equipment locations.

If emergency support contracts are not in place with vendors, the agency procurement office should immediately begin contacting vendors and equipment manufacturers who may be able to help. Often, local vendors are overwhelmed, but the original equipment manufacturer may know of resources available elsewhere.

For governmental entities, technical assistance is often available from:

> State Office of Emergency Management
> Statewide Interoperability Coordinator (SWIC)
> National Guard Communications Units
> Federal Emergency Management Agency (for declared disasters)
> DHS Office of Emergency Communications
> Nearby military bases—Many commanders have authority to assist
>   civilian agencies in time of emergency
> Amateur Radio Emergency Service®, ARES
> Military Auxiliary Radio System (MARS)

For nonprofit organizations, certain limited assistance in troubleshooting and restoring primary systems may be obtained from the above sources, but NGOs should also consider these resources first:

> Amateur Radio Emergency Service®, ARES
> Community Emergency Response Team (CERT)
> Local Amateur Radio Clubs
> Other nonprofits who may operate similar systems, such as the
>   Salvation Army Team Emergency Radio Network (SATERN)
> National or State Voluntary Organizations Active in Disaster (VOAD)

Business and Industry are expected to find commercial sources of assistance, unless their outage directly impacts public safety, in which case the business should contact the local government office of emergency management or local Emergency Operations Center for guidance. Under certain circumstances, it is also possible for business to receive assistance from ARES.

Assessing the Current Situation

Initial Damage Assessment

Initial damage assessment begins with an inventory of what systems are working, what is degraded, and what has failed.

What is the impact on the community of each failure?

Is the situation stable or is it dynamic?

Is there time for a careful technical review, or do you need to make decisions with only the information you have?

Can you provide a minimum acceptable level of service to your customers with what you have?

If not, can you devolve your responsibilities to another organization?

If devolution is not possible, what will be the end result of your degraded capabilities?

How long can your community tolerate the degradation?

Communicate your findings up your chain of command promptly, with recommendations and resource requests to follow as you continue your assessment.

Determining Immediate Resource Needs

Consider the criticality of each degraded system in order to determine restoration priority.

What is the impact on the community of each system failure?

Can working systems be reprogrammed to support a higher priority need?

As a minimum, you also need to consider the dynamic impact of the events that caused the disruption: Are conditions getting better or worse? What is expected for the next 24 hours?

What are the fastest repairs and who can make them?

What are the risks to the workers?

Does the benefit of restoration justify the risk?

What backup systems can be mobilized until repairs are complete?

What auxiliary capabilities, such as ARES, can be brought in, and how will they be used?

Who pays, and how much?

Prioritizing Resource Requirements

Of the available staff, who is the most technically knowledgeable about your system of systems? If possible, put them in charge of restoration and give them the authority to get the job done.

Everything cannot be done at once. Usually, the following guide helps to prioritize:

> Priority One: Systems with critical impact that can be restored rapidly

> Priority Two: Non-critical systems that can be restored rapidly, then reprogrammed to support a critical need.

> Priority Three: Critical systems requiring major repairs

> Priority Four: Non-critical systems that can be restored with major effort, then reprogrammed to support a critical need.

> Priority Five: Critical systems requiring total replacement or extensive repairs

> Priority Six: All others

Ordering and Managing Resources

Who has the authority to order resources? If it is you, then order what you need in priority sequence.

If you do not have ordering authority, make a list of the resources you need immediately and communicate it up your chain of command.

Once resources are ordered, document everything related to the tasking: What was ordered, when it arrived, where it went, how it was used, and when it was released.

Resource tracking is vitally important, whether the resource is equipment, people or something else. As a minimum, your finance office will need to pay the bill, and you will need to justify the costs.

Whenever resources aren't in use, they should be assigned to a staging area for immediate dispatch.

When no longer needed, resources should be released so they can be used elsewhere.

Your Emergency Communications Plan

Your emergency communications plan, if not pre-made, needs to be drafted quickly so that everyone can make the most of available resources.

ICS Form 205 is designed to ease this task.

Individuals who have been specifically trained in developing emergency communications plans are known in the Incident Command System by their resource identifier "COML," or Communications Unit Leader. Some COMT, Communications Unit Technicians, also have this training.

If you need a COML or COMT, contact your county or state emergency management office or Incident Command System (ICS) ordering point.

If you order a COML or COMT through ICS, keep in mind the resource typing system: Type I COMLs are certified to handle catastrophic events; Type II COMLs are certified for very large events; while Type III COMLs can handle complex multijurisdictional, but relatively localized emergencies.

If you do not have a COML or COMT available, you may have to develop the communications plan yourself.

The following page shows an example of an emergency communications plan, and the page afterwards provides you a blank ICS Form 205.

Important note: The ICS Form 205 is an intentionally brief communications plan, outlining only the most critical information needed to set up and operate radio nets. Success depends on communications technicians and users who are trained in reading and implementing this type of communications plan.

By utilizing standardized terminology and forms, the Incident Command System aims to reduce confusion during emergencies, and this principle applies particularly to the Incident Radio Communications Plan, the ICS Form 205.

ICS 205: Sample Incident Radio Communications Plan

INCIDENT RADIO COMMUNICATIONS PLAN		Incident Name: DELTA		Date/Time Prepared 4/12/2006 1930				Operational Period Date/Time 4/12/2006 2000 To 4/13/2006 0600	
Ch #	Function	Channel Name/Trunked Radio System Talkgroup	Assignment	RX freq N or W	RX Tone/NAC	TX freq N or W	Tx Tone/NAC	Mode	Remarks
1	COMMAND	COMMON	Command	154.9500 W	None	158.7750 W	136.5	A	Repeater on High Hill
2	COMMAND	GOLD STAR	Command	460.1000 W	None	465.1000 W	179.9	A	Patched to Ch. 1 via Gateway @ICP
3	TACTICAL	PD TAC 1	Law Branch	155.5200 W	136.5	155.5200 W	136.5	A	
4	TACTICAL	FD TAC 1	Fire Branch	154.3250 W	141.8	154.3250 W	141.8	A	
5	TACTICAL	EMS TAC 1	EMS Branch	(Jonesville 800 MHz. Trunked Radio System)				A	
6									

5. Prepared by (Communications Unit)
J. Powell, COML (800) 555-1212 cell

Incident Location
County **Johnson** State **NC** Latitude **39-48-12** N Longitude **115-00-05** W

The convention calls for frequency lists to show four digits after the decimal place, followed by either an "N" or a "W", depending on whether the frequency is narrow or wide band. Mode refers to either "A" or "D" indicating analog or digital (Project 25)

ICS 205-Draft 041106

ICS 205: Blank Incident Radio Communications Plan

INCIDENT RADIO COMMUNICATIONS PLAN	1. Incident Name	2. Date/Time Prepared	3. Operational Period (Date/Time)

4. BASIC RADIO CHANNEL UTILIZATION

System / Cache	Channel	Function	Frequency	Assignment	Remarks

5. Prepared By: (Communications Unit)

ICS 205 8/96

Emergency Communications Systems

The following matrix displays the main characteristics and most significant differences among various emergency communications systems which may be available to you.

Mention of specific brand names are for illustration only and does not imply indorsement of nor criticism of any specific company or service.

Emergency Communications Systems Comparison		
Common Carrier Voice and Data Communications		
System*	**Advantages**	**Disadvantages**
Wireline Voice and Data	Relatively Low cost	Vulnerable infrastructure (Cable, fiber, copper wire)
Wireless Cellular, PCS, LTE, Mobile Data Terminals	Portability Flexibility Moderate cost Restorability	Vulnerable cell sites May use wireline Congestion
Satellite-Fixed Service COMSAT HUGHES NET	Reliability	High cost Usually fixed antenna Speed limits Congestion Space weather impact
Satellite- Portable/Mobile INMARSAT GATR BGAN	Reliability Mobility Portability	High cost Speed limits Congestion Space weather impact
Satellite- Portable/Mobile HUGHES NET DATASTAR	Reliability Mobility	High cost Speed limits Congestion Space weather impact
Satellite- Fixed/Mobile IRIDIUM GLOBALSTAR THURAYA	Reliability Portability	High cost Speed limits Congestion Space weather impact
Satellite- Fixed/Mobile SPOT	Reliability Portability Emergency alerts Relatively low cost	Text only Limited messaging Space weather impact

Land Mobile Radio Voice and Data Communications		
System*	Advantages	Disadvantages
Licensed Public Safety, Business, Itinerant	Under your control Predictable cost Flexible Reliable Expandable Common equipment	Vulnerable sites License limitations Time to repair
MURS Multi-Use Radio System	No license required Very low cost Flexible Reliable Expandable Common equipment	1-3 km limited range No repeaters No data
GMRS General Mobile Radio System	Under your control Very low cost Flexible Reliable Expandable Repeaters available	1-3 km range without repeater License required Limited business use No government use No data
FRS Family Radio System	No license required Under your control Very low cost Flexible Reliable Expandable	<1 km range No repeaters No data
ARES® Amateur Radio Emergency Service	Flexibility No direct cost Voice, data, video High Speed Multimedia Local & global coverage	Business use restrictions Volunteer limitations
Maritime Radio Service	Relatively low cost Mobility Portability Telephone patch Operator support	License required Marine/inland waterways only
Military Auxiliary Radio System (MARS)	Mobility Portability Local & global coverage Voice and data Encryption available	Requires DOD coordination Other missions are primary

*Typical service providers are shown for illustration only.

Emergency Resources

There is no substitute for your organization compiling its own emergency resource contact list.

Your list should include every key supplier, all sources of mutual aid, and all organizations in a position to assist you in emergency.

The outlines on the following pages may assist. It is recommended that you edit each listing with specific information about each resource. Don't forget to include specific contact information.

Repeater Site Destroyed by Wildfire, 2012
Photo: Shutterstock

Wireline Carriers

Wireline carriers (telephone companies) usually have mutual aid agreements with neighboring utilities in case of emergency. Normally their switching centers have robust backup power systems, including generators. Their chief vulnerabilities are (1) Single points of failure such as switching centers and (2) Extensive wiring infrastructure that is exposed to disruption. Restoration is very labor intensive.

Depending on your contract with the wireline carrier, they may or may not be responsible for the wiring, switching systems, and telephone instruments in your facility. Where the telephone wiring enters your facility, there is a point, usually within an outdoor utility box, that the carrier refers to as the "Dmarc" or demarcation point. Everything outside that point is their responsibility. Everything inside that point is your responsibility unless you have contracted with the telephone company for maintenance.

Line Load Control is a semi-automatic process that protects switching equipment by shutting down subscriber access whenever the system becomes overloaded. In other words, customers do not get a dial tone. You may be able to arrange with the carrier to exempt critical office numbers as well as the home telephones of emergency-essential staff.

Every critical line in the U.S. should be considered Telecommunications Service Priority (TSP) status. Refer to the section on TSP.

Government Emergency Telecommunications System (GETS) calling cards should be considered for key personnel whose duties are critical to public safety, security, health and welfare. Refer to the section on GETS.

Information about your wireline carrier:

Name of Company:_____

Primary Point of Contact: _____

After-Hours Emergency Contact: _____

Email or Web Contact Form: _____

Summarize their responsibilities under your contract:_____

_____

_____

Wireless Carriers

Most locations in the U.S. and Canada are served by multiple wireless carriers. Mobile phones usually are linked to a specific wireless network cannot work on competing networks, although there some exceptions. Towers often support antennas for many if not all wireless competitors, which means that multiple carriers may be affected if there is damage to a tower.

Cell sites may or may not have backup power sufficient to last for an extended period of time. Remote sites may be difficult to service.

The larger wireless carriers have extensive disaster response capabilities which they usually deploy on their own initiative when needed. These include mobile customer support centers, a variety of mobile cellular sites, and in some cases satellite terminals. They may also be able to respond to your requests for expanded or restored service in specific areas.

A serious challenge in setting up mobile cellular sites is the ability to access the high speed cable or fiber infrastructure from that site. If cable and fiber have been disrupted, it is likely that cell service will also be impacted.

Generally, it is a good idea for critical communications centers to have equipment that will access all wireless carriers providing service in the area.

Wireless Priority Service (WPS) should be considered for key personnel whose duties are critical to public safety, security, health and welfare. Refer to the section on WPS.

Information about your wireless carrier:

Name of Company:_____

Primary Point of Contact: _____

After-Hours Emergency Contact: _____

Email or Web Contact Form: _____

Summarize their responsibilities under your contract:_____

_____

_____

List contacts for other wireless carriers in your area:

_____

Internet Service Providers

Internet Service Providers (ISPs) offer a wide range of connectivity options and features, including direct broadband, such as T1 circuits, DSL, cable, wireless point-to-point, 3G/4G cellular, and satellite service, among others.

Organizations should consider obtaining internet service from one than more vendor, and using more than one type of infrastructure for their ciritical systems. Additionally, having a standby capability, such as satellite internet, and knowing how to obtain emergency service are important considerations for emergency communications planning.

Generally, ISPs are not regulated by the FCC the same way as common carriers (such as phone companies). While there are some federal regulations, most regulation is left up to the states and local government. Organizations should be familiar with the regulations that pertain to each ISP, particularly regarding requirements for service restoration following an outage, or lack thereof.

Information about your internet service provider:

Name of Company:_____

Primary Point of Contact: _____

After-Hours Emergency Contact: _____

Email or Web Contact Form: _____

Summarize their responsibilities under your contract:_____

_____

_____

List contacts for other providers in your area:

Mobile or Portable Satellite Service Providers

Internet access is available through direct satellite links. High speed broadband is available, but the cost is exceptionally high, and your satellite dish will need to be large.

Lower speed broadband is available at moderate cost, using smaller dishes.

Mobile and portable service is also available.

As a rule, systems using fixed dishes need a certified installer to set up and commission the equipment before it can be used. Normally, equipment is specific to a satellite service and cannot be used on another satellite vendor's network, although certain retailers are actually branding an underlying satellite service with their own name, and some mobility may be possible to another retailer using the same wholesale satellite service.

Some satellite telephone services allow a low speed data connection through the satellite phone handset or base station.

A major caution is that many satellite service providers impose rigid caps on the amount of data that can be exchanged by a user within each month's billing cycle. Once that data cap is reached, the speed of the satellite connection is throttled back to a much slower speed. As a result, when the service is needed most during an emergency, the caps are reached and the service slows to a small fraction of its usual bandwidth. Be sure to confirm your limits with your service provider and determine if there are any provisions for obtaining more bandwidth during an emergency.

Information about your satellite service provider:

Name of Company:_____

Primary Point of Contact: _____

After-Hours Emergency Contact: _____

Email or Web Contact Form: _____

Summarize their responsibilities under your contract:_____

_____

_____

List contacts for other satellite service providers:
_____

Government Emergency Telecommunications Service (GETS)

GETS is an emergency telephone communications program sponsored by the U.S. Department of Homeland Security.

Individuals with a valid need for priority calling during emergencies may be eligible for a GETS calling card. GETS works with traditional, wired telephones.

If a dial tone can be accessed, GETS should provide priority access in most cases, but GETS does not preempt existing calls.

For more information about GETS and to see if you qualify for for a GETS calling card if you are a non-federal entity, contact the communications officer in your State office of emergency management. Federal agencies should contact your national security emergency preparedness liaison or regional coordinator for the DHS Office of Emergency Communications for guidance.

General information about GETS is available at:

http://www.dhs.gov/government-emergency-telecommunications-service-gets

Wireless Priority Service (WPS)

WPS is the wireless emergency telephone communications program sponsored by the U.S. Department of Homeland Security.

Individuals with a valid need for priority calling during emergencies may be eligible for WPS. Under WPS, a cell phone number may receive priority calling service..

If a cell carrier can be accessed, WPS should provide priority access in most cases, but WPS does not preempt existing calls.

WPS may not provide priority access under the LTE development of the cellular architecture, according to some wireless carriers, due to technical issues. However, WPS should function on traditional cell networks until LTE deployment.

There is a monthly charge for WPS designation on a cell phone. This charge appears on the regular billing statement for the phone.

For more information about WPS and to see if you qualify for the program if you are a non-federal entity, contact the communications officer in your State office of emergency management. Federal agencies should contact your national security emergency preparedness liaison or regional coordinator for the DHS Office of Emergency Communications for guidance.

General information about WPS is available at:

https://www.dhs.gov/wireless-priority-service-wps

Telecommunications Service Priority (TSP)

TSP is a special designation for telecommunications circuits in the United States indicating that they must be provisioned rapidly or restored ahead of normal circuits following disruption.

Restoration TSP must be ordered ahead of time. It cannot be ordered once circuits are disrupted.

It is extremely important that national security, emergency preparedness, and critical public safety circuits be designated with restoration TSP, or their restoration will simply occur at the convenience of the service provider, rather than on a high-priority basis.

Service providers charge a moderate fee for TSP.

To inquire about eligibility for TSP for non-federal entities, contact the communications officer in your State's office of emergency management. Federal agencies should contact your national security emergency preparedness liaison or regional coordinator for the DHS Office of Emergency Communications for guidance.

More information about TSP is available at:

http://www.dhs.gov/telecommunications-service-priority-tsp

Mobile or Portable Repeaters

Mobile or portable repeaters may be an option for emergency replacement for failed repeaters, or to supplement the existing system in time of emergency.

Mobile or portable repeaters require a license from the Federal Communications Commission (non-federal entities) or the National Telecommunications and Information Agency (for federal agencies).

Amateur radio portable repeaters do not require specific licensing other than for their control operator, and can generally be activated after relatively rapid frequency coordination.

In extreme emergencies, a request may be made to the FCC for Special Temporary Authority (STA) for mobile or portable repeaters on public service and commercial frequencies.

There are potential problems with mobile or portable repeaters, which must be taken into account:

- Unintentional interference with other users
- Less than desired signal coverage due to adverse terrain or compromises in repeater location
- Difficulty linking with existing system

Mobile or portable repeaters may be rented from a variety of service providers.

During Presidentially declared disasters and some other emergencies, FEMA may be able to provide temporary repeaters to governmental entities.

For more information about Special Temporary Authority:

http://wireless.fcc.gov/services/index.htm?job=operations_3&id=industrial_bu siness

Military Auxiliary Radio System (MARS)

In the U.S., each military service operates a MARS program for support of Department of Defense emergency communications. Canada has a similar program.

Primary mission of MARS is backup command and control communications for the military. Secondary missions include support to other governmental agencies in time of emergency; health and welfare messaging for service members; technical training and other missions as assigned.

While there is broad cooperation and mutual support among the service branch MARS organizations, administratively each service has a chain of command extending from service headquarters, through regional and state directors, to the individual member.

Information about service MARS programs is available from:

Army MARS: http://www.netcom.army.mil/mars/links.aspx

Navy/Marine Corps MARS: http://navymars.org/

Air Force MARS: http://afmars.org/

Information about MARS Points of Contact in your area:

Army MARS: _____

Navy/Marine Corps MARS: _____

USAF MARS: _____

Summarize their capabilities and procedures:_____

_____

_____

Shared Resources High Frequency Program (SHARES)

The SHARES HF Radio Program, administered by the Department of Homeland Security's Office of Emergency Communications (OEC), provides an additional means for users with a national security and emergency preparedness mission to communicate when landline and cellular communications are unavailable.

SHARES members use existing HF radio resources to coordinate and transmit messages needed to perform critical functions, including those areas related to leadership, safety, maintenance of law and order, finance, and public health.

For additional information: http://www.dhs.gov/shares

Point of Contact for SHARES: _____

Summarize their capabilities and procedures:_____

_____

_____

Civil Air Patrol (CAP)

In the U.S., the Civil Air Patrol (CAP) is the official auxiliary of the U.S. Air Force. CAP can provide airborne logistics, command-control, communications, search and rescue, and a variety of other services in time of emergency.

CAP operates a robust system of nationwide emergency communications nets.

Some CAP units have the capability of aerial video and infrared capabilities, and most units can provide airborne radio relay platforms.

CAP is organized from a national headquarters, through regions and states, to local units. The state level organization is a "Wing," whose commander has considerable authority for approving support activities.

It is highly recommended that local emergency managers maintain current contact information for their CAP Wing.

For additional information: http://www.gocivilairpatrol.com/

Point of Contact for CAP: _____

Summarize their capabilities and procedures:_____

_____

_____

Coast Guard Auxiliary

In the U.S. and Canada, both nation's Coast Guard Auxiliary provides exceptional support for marine safety, public education, and emergency communications.

Coast Guard Auxiliary units have access to local, national, and international communications capabilities in time of emergency.

Coast Guard Auxiliary communications officers are highly trained and many are COML certified. Most are experienced in providing liaison with active Coast Guard units as well as Army, Navy and Air Force units involved with Military Support to Civil Authority (MSCA) missions.

It is highly recommended that local emergency managers maintain an emergency contact list for nearby Coast Guard Auxiliary squadrons.

For additional information:

U.S. Coast Guard Auxiliary: http://www.cgaux.org/

    and: http://www.uscg.mil/auxiliary/default.asp

Canadian Coast Guard Auxiliary: http://ccga-gcac.ca/

Point of Contact for CGA: _____

Summarize their capabilities and procedures:_____

_____

_____

Amateur Radio Auxiliary Communications

In most but not all countries, amateur radio operators are permitted to provide disaster emergency communications support to governmental agencies, relief organizations, and in some cases the public.

In the U.S., the Amateur Radio Emergency Service® (ARES®) is the principal organization within which emergency response teams are usually formed.

In some states, an Auxiliary Communications organization may be formed separate from, or in conjunction with ARES®.

The Radio Amateur Civil Emergency Service (RACES) is a category of amateur auxiliary communications service which states and local governments may choose to use because of its availability in time of national security emergency.

ARES® is overseen nationally by the ARRL—The national association for amateur radio (www.arrl.org), and managed by Section Emergency Coordinators at the State level, and District Emergency Coordinators at the county or local level.

Emergency managers are encouraged to contact their ARES emergency coordinators and incorporate ARES resources into emergency response plans.

Additional information about ARES®: www.arrl.org

Point of Contact for ARES: _____

Summarize their capabilities and procedures:_____

_____

_____

Point of Contact for RACES:

_____

Summarize their capabilities and procedures:_____

_____

_____

Communications Equipment Manufacturers

Having direct contact with the manufacturer of your critical systems may be very important following a disaster which impacts intermediate wholesalers or your local vendor. Manufacturers are often able to arrange emergency support from across the country or around the world.

Documenting their emergency contact information is highly recommended.

Information about your equipment manufacturer:

Name of Company:_____

Primary Point of Contact: _____

After-Hours Emergency Contact: _____

Email or Web Contact Form: _____

Summarize they might provide:_____

_____

_____

List contacts for other equipment providers:

Communications Equipment Rental

In an emergency, you may need to rent additional equipment or lease replacements for systems damaged in a disaster.

Having a directory of resource providers will be very helpful.

To customize your list, you may wish to begin with a review of articles and ads in trade magazines or a visit with vendors at emergency management conferences, as well as contact with local suppliers.

Documenting their emergency contact information is highly recommended.

Information about sources for equipment rental:

Name of Company:_____

Primary Point of Contact: _____

After-Hours Emergency Contact: _____

Email or Web Contact Form: _____

Summarize they might provide:_____

_____

_____

List contacts for other equipment providers:

Portable Emergency Power Generator Rental

It may not be possible to rent portable power generation equipment on short notice unless you have a prior relationship with the vendor.

Following a disaster, one of the first resources to be exhausted is the local and possibly regional supply of standby generators.

If you need additional or backup resources, the best approach is to have a standing contract for delivery of generators should commercial power fail.

Otherwise, you should attempt to establish a relationship with potential providers of rental equipment.

Documenting their emergency contact information is highly recommended.

Information about sources for power generation equipment rental:

Name of Company:_____

Primary Point of Contact: _____

After-Hours Emergency Contact: _____

Email or Web Contact Form: _____

Summarize they might provide:_____

_____

_____

List contacts for other equipment providers:

Fuel Delivery Services

It may not be possible to obtain fuel on short notice unless you have a prior relationship with the supplier.

If you need emergency-support fuel deliveries the best approach is to have a standing contract for delivery.

You should attempt to establish a relationship with potential providers of fuel in an emergency.

Documenting their emergency contact information is highly recommended.

Information about sources for fuel delivery:

Name of Company:_____

Primary Point of Contact: _____

After-Hours Emergency Contact: _____

Email or Web Contact Form: _____

Summarize they might provide:_____

_____

_____

List contacts for other fuel providers:

Tower Repair and Climbing Services

Tower climbing and repair require specialized skills and equipment. If you do not have an established relationship with a provider of this support, then it may be difficult to impossible to obtain timely assistance following a disaster.

Documenting their emergency contact information is highly recommended.

Information about sources for tower climbing and repair:

Name of Company:_____

Primary Point of Contact: _____

After-Hours Emergency Contact: _____

Email or Web Contact Form: _____

Summarize they might provide:_____

_____

_____

List contacts for other tower maintenance resources:

Part Three: Technical References

Computer Connectors: RS-232

RS-232 Connectors (DB25 and DB9)

"Front" refers to the ends with the pins; "rear" refers to the end with the cable. The following is a view of the pins, looking at the front of the female connector (rear of male):

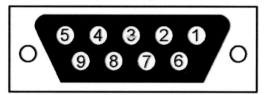

same for DB25, except top pins 13 - 1, bottom 25 - 14 (left to right)

DB9	DB25	Signal
1	8	Carrier Detect
2	3	Receive Data
3	2	Transmit Data*
4	20	Data Terminal Ready*
5	1,7	Ground**
6	6	Data Set Ready
7	4	Request to Send*
8	5	Clear to Send
9	22	Ring Indicator
* An output from the computer to the outside world.		
** On the DB25, 1 is the protective ground, 7 is the signal ground.		

Computer Cables: RJ-45 Connections

		T568A (less common)		T568B (more common)	
Pin	Pair	Color	Name	Color	Name
1	2	white/green	RecvData+	white/orange	TxData +
2	2	green	RecvData-	orange	TxData -
3	3	white/orange	TxData +	white/green	RecvData+
4	1	blue		blue	
5	1	white/blue		white/blue	
6	3	orange	TxData -	green	RecvData-
7	4	white/brown		white/brown	
8	4	brown		brown	

Note that the odd pin numbers are always the white-with-stripe color.

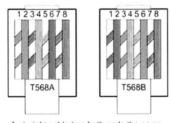

A straight cable has both ends the same –
both T568A (older standard) or both
T568B (newer standard).
A crossover cable has one end wired as
T568A, the other as T568B.

Telephone Plug Standards

Pin numbers are from left to right, holding the plug with the contacts up and looking at the side that does not have the spring clip. "T" and "R" indicate "Tip" and "Ring".

Pin	RJ25	RJ14	RJ11
1	T3		
2	T2	T2	
3	R1	R1	R1
4	T1	T1	T1
5	R2	R2	
6	R3		

Circuit	Twisted-Pair Colors	25-Pair Colors	Solid Colors
T1	White/Blue	White/Blue	Green
R1	Blue	Blue/White	Red
T2	White/Orange	White/Orange	Black
R2	Orange	Orange/White	Yellow
T3	White/Green	White/Green	White
R3	Green	Green/White	Blue
T4	White/Brown	White/Brown	Orange
R4	Brown	Brown/White	Brown

Telephone Frame Room Standards

Tip, Ring	Tip Color (reverse for Ring)	50 Pin Position	66 or 110 Block Position
1	White/Blue	26,1	1,2
2	White/Orange	27,2	3,4
3	White/Green	28,3	5,6
4	White/Brown	29,4	7,8
5	White/Slate	30,5	9,10
6	Red/Blue	31,6	11,12
7	Red/Orange	32,7	13,14
8	Red/Green	33,8	15,16
9	Red/Brown	34,9	17,18
10	Red/Slate	35,10	19,20
11	Black/Blue	36,11	21,22
12	Black/Orange	37,12	23,24
13	Black/Green	38,13	25,26
14	Black/Brown	39,14	27,28
15	Black/Slate	40,15	29,30
16	Yellow/Blue	41,16	31,32
17	Yellow/Orange	42,17	33,34
18	Yellow/Green	43,18	35,36
19	Yellow/Brown	44,19	37,38
20	Yellow/Slate	45,20	39,40
21	Violet/Blue	46,21	41,42
22	Violet/Orange	47,22	43,44
23	Violet/Green	48,23	45,46
24	Violet/Brown	49,24	47,48
25	Violet/Slate	50,25	49,50

Glossary

ACU – Audio Control Unit, widely used to tie together different radio networks that are otherwise incompatible. The ACU allows audio from each network to be heard on the other.

AED – Automatic External Defibrillator

AES – Advanced Encryption Standard, based on 256 bit encryption.

Air Card – A radio-modem card that plugs into a computer, providing broadband access over a wireless carrier's network.

Air Gap – Physical separation between systems, generally requiring human action to transfer information from one system to another. This may be a preplanned security feature, or it may result from incompatible systems.

AGL – Air to Ground Link

Aldis Lamp – A signal light used to send messages by blinking, widely used by navies and installed in air traffic control towers and some aircraft for communications when radios cannot be used.

All Hazards Radio – Previously known as NOAA weather radio. The system is operated by the NOAA's National Weather Service to transmit weather information to the public, but is also an important part of the Emergency Alert System/Integrated Public Alerting and Warning System. Transmitter sites cover most metro areas of the U.S., and are equipped with EAS encoders/decoders for automatic transmission of priority messages to the public.

AM – Amplitude Modulation

AMBE+2 – The voice encoder (vocoder) method specified by the P25 interoperability standard.

Amateur Radio Service – The amateur radio service is a formally designated service by the International Telecommunications Union (ITU). Internationally coordinated frequencies and common operating practices allow for very flexible communications around the world. In general, licensed amateur radio operators may not be compensated either directly or indirectly for their services, but may provide emergency communications in support of disasters with considerable latitude. The Amateur Radio Service is regulated in the U.S. by the Federal Communications Commission and in Canada by Industry Canada.

AMR – Aeronautical Mobile Radio

AMPS – Advanced Mobile Phone System, an analog format that is obsolete in North America.

Analog – As used for radio, analog modulation varies a transmitter signal in direct proportion to the sound being sent, as opposed to a digital system, which converts the sound into a stream of bits that vary in pattern but not strength nor frequency as they are sent.

ANI/ALI – Automatic Number Identification / Automatic Location Information

APCO – The Association of Public Safety Communications Officers

APCO-16 – A radio trunking standard largely replaced by APCO-25 (P25)

APCO-25 – One of the principal radio interoperability standards in the U.S.. See P25.

APRS – Automatic Packet Reporting System

ARES -- Amateur Radio Emergency Service. In many countries, ARES or a similar organization is the organization of amateur radio operators dedicated to assisting the public and response agencies during emergencies. In the United Kingdom, for instance, the comparable organization is known as RAYNET.

ARL – An system of brevity codes used by amateur radio operators to speed up handling of messages

ARRL – American Radio Relay League

Bandwidth – Technically, bandwidth refers to the range of radio frequencies used by the system. In practice, the term usually refers to the throughput speed of a data system. In most cases, the broader the bandwidth, the higher the speed.

Baudot Code – A signaling system used mainly in teletype systems that allowed remote teleprinting.

Broadband –A generic term generally meaning high speed data.

BPL - Broadband over Power Line, which is a system that uses power lines as the transmission medium for high speed data communications. Disadvantages of the system are high operational costs, limited service capabilities, and radio interference to other users.

CAD – Computer Aided Dispatch

CAD – Computer Aided Drawing

CAI – Common Air Interface is a set of technical standards intended to make it possible for radio equipment from different manufactures to work together on a digital radio network.

Calling Frequency or Channel – A designated frequency or channel used to initially establish communications. Once the parties are linked, they move to a Traffic Channel or another frequency, keeping the calling channel clear.

CAP – Civil Air Patrol

CAP – Common Alerting Protocol, as used in the Integrated Public Alert and Warning System and associated systems.

CB – Citizens Band

CDMA – Code Division Multiplex is one of the many coding schemes used in digital systems to increase speed and message capacity. It is one of the four mutually incompatible methods used by wireless telephone providers. In the U.S., CDMA is used by Verizon, Sprint and U.S. Cellular.

Central Office – The local switching center for a telephone company

CEPT – European Conference of Postal and Telecommunications Administrations, from the French acronym for the official name *Conférence européenne des administrations des postes et des télécommunications*. Many non-European countries, including the U.S., Australia, New Zealand, and Canada, have entered into important treaty relationships with CEPT, allowing increased interoperability and in some cases reciprocal operating privileges among the participating countries.

CIAB – Cell in a Box

Coax – Coaxial cable is used as a feeder cable for radio antennas, as well as providing local and long distance "cable" service.

COLT – Cell on Light Truck

COW – Cell on Wheels (usually a trailer)

COML – Communications Unit Leader (ICS Identifier)

COMT – Communications Technician (ICS Identifier)

Command Frequency or Channel – The designated frequency for incident command communications, as opposed to operational, logistical and tactical matters, which are handled on different channels.

Channel – A radio frequency, usually programmed into a radio with a channel identification name or number.

Co-channel Interference – Inadvertent interference between users on the same frequency or channel.

Cradlepoint – A proprietary service that provides broadband over wireless, specially marketed as an emergency backup system.

Crossband – Transmission and reception on vastly different radio bands, usually done to reduce co-channel interference.

CTCSS – Continuous Tone-Coded Squelch System is the inclusion of a subaudible tone on a radio transmission in order to signal other radios and repeaters that a station on their own system is transmitting. It is one of the methods for establishing semi-closed radio nets and reducing interference.

CW – Continuous Wave technically refers to the type of signal generated by a modern transmitter. In common usage, CW generally refers to one of the most efficient methods of transmitting Morse Code by radio. CW commonly means on-and-off keying of the transmitter, so that little or no power is consumed between bursts of signal.

DACS – Digital Access Cross Connect is a method for digitizing analog signals and sending them across a high volume digital system. This method is commonly used in telephone systems.

DCS – Digital Code Squelch uses a string of characters at the beginning of a digital radio transmission to establish links between similarly programmed radios, reducing interference and keeping user's radios quiet except when transmissions are intended from them.

DES – Digital Encryption Standard is based on 56 bit encryption. Improvements include 2-key triple DES and 3-key triple DES.

DMR – Digital Mobile Radio is one of the encoding standards for digital radio. Some manufacturers have developed proprietary subsets of this standard.

Doppler Shift – A change in frequency caused by the motion of a moving object, such as the changed pitch of the whistle when a train passes. Doppler shift is used in radar to determine speed. Doppler shift also causes a problem for communications system, particularly when using orbital satellites, as the satellite frequency is constantly changing.

D-STAR – An open digital radio standard developed by the Japan Amateur Radio League and widely used, particularly in radios with the ICOM brand.

Duplex – Transmitting and receiving at the same time. Most desk phones are duplex. Most handheld radio transceivers are simplex, mean that you usually push a button to transmit, then release to listen.

E-911—Enhanced 9-1-1 system, which normally includes Automatic Number Identification and Automatic Location Information (ANI/ALI) for the dispatcher.

EAG – Emergency Action Guide

EAS – Emergency Alert System

Echolink – A popular method of linking amateur radio stations and repeaters over the internet, allowing global communications from a handheld radio.

EDACS – Enhanced Digital Access Communications System is a proprietary radio trunking and linking system developed by General Electric and currently used on Ericcson and Harris equipment. The protocol is not inherently interoperable with other proprietary systems, although some audio linking systems allow for limited exchange of voice and data communications.

EDGE – Enhanced Data for GSM Evolution is a proprietary protocol for data over wireless networks, largely replaced by High Speed Packet Access (HSPA) and other faster protocols.

EMCOMM – Emergency Communications

Encoding – In communications, this is the process of applying a signaling or modulation scheme to raw data or voice so that it can be efficiently transmitted. Encoding does not necessarily imply the intent to obscure.

Encryption – The process of obscuring or concealing communications for secrecy or privacy.

ESF – Emergency Support Function

EVDO – Evolution Data Optimized, a proprietary form of 3G (third generation) wireless service using Code Division Multiple Access (CDMA) coding.

FAX – Facsimile, or transmission images

FDMA – Frequency Division Multiple Access is one of the three most commonly used processes to put more radio signals into a single channel. The other two are Code Division Multiple Access (CDMA) and Time Domain Multiple Access.

Fiber or Fiber Optic cable carries extremely data at extremely high speeds over great distances using light.

FiOS – Fiber Optic Service is a proprietary term referring to internet service over fiber optic service.

FNARS – FEMA National Radio System

Frequency Authorization in the U.S. is issued by the Federal Communications Commission (FCC) for the public, business, broadcasters, and all governmental bodies except for federal agencies, which obtain their authorizations from the National Telecommunications and Information Agency (NTIA).

FRS – Family Radio Service

FCC – Federal Communications Commission

FM – Frequency Modulation

FOG – Field Operations Guide

FSTV – Fast Scan Television

GATR – A proprietary portable satellite communications system.

Geosynchronous Satellite – An earth satellite whose orbit maintains a relatively fixed position in the sky, which can provide a continuous communications path. The three main disadvantages are (1) Very high cost because of the 40,000 km orbit, (2) Relatively high power/large antennas needed by earth stations due to the distance, and (3) Lack of coverage for the polar regions, and seriously impaired coverage for any location beyond 60 degrees north or south latitude.

GETS – Government Emergency Telecommunications System

GMRS – General Mobile Radio Service

GPS – Global Positioning System

Ground Plane – Generally refers to a vertical antenna over solid metal or wires, which generally directs radio signals toward the horizon in all directions.

Ground Wave – A radio signal usually on lower frequencies that essentially hugs the ground as it propagates, making communications possible for dozens of kilometers during the day, and about 200-300 kilometers at night, depending on transmitter power and antennas.

GSM – Global System for Mobile Communications, the cellular telephone standard throughout the European Union, which is also used by AT+T Wireless and T-Mobile in the U.S.

GTOR – Golay-Coded Teletype Over Radio is a standard used for many data transmissions.

Ham – Amateur Radio Operator

Hardline – A type of coaxial cable that is relatively efficient at carrying radio signals up to and including low microwave frequencies. These cables are heavy and difficult to bend.

HEO – High Earth Orbit

Hertz – Unit of measurement for one cycle per second

HF – High Frequency

HSPA – High Speed Packet Access is a proprietary protocol for data over wireless networks.

ICS – Incident Command System

IARP – International Amateur Radio Permit is a treaty arrangement among most, but not all, countries in South and North America providing a process by which amateur radio operators licensed in one country can obtain operating privileges in another.

IMBE –   Improved Multi-Band Excitation Vocoder

IMS – Incident Management System

Industry Canada – The Canadian agency responsible for regulating telecommunications in Canada and issuing radio licenses.

Intermod or Intermodulation – The usually undesirable result when two or more radio signals combine in a circuit, resulting in interference.

Ionosphere – The upper level of earth's atmosphere that reflects radio signals and permits global radio communications.

IPAWS – Integrated Public Alert and Warning System

Iridium® – A commercial satellite communications system

IRLP – Internet Radio Linking Project

IARU – The International Amateur Radio Union

ISP – Internet Service Provider

ITU – International Telecommunications Union

JARL – Japanese Amateur Radio League

LEO – Low Earth Orbit

LF – Low Frequency

Li-Fi -- Light Fidelity. An emerging technology similar in concept to Wi-Fi which uses the visible light spectrum rather than radio waves to connect portable devices. One promising application is to provide connectivity for a network within a secure environment, with minimal risk that communications can be intercepted from the outside.

Line-A – A boundary line stretching from Maine to Washington State at about 46 degrees North latitude (44° N in Maine), roughly parallel to the Canadian border, intended to protect Canadian radio systems from U.S. interference. Canada has a similar boundary line to protect U.S. systems. By treaty, radio transmitters in certain frequency bands within these border regions require both country's coordination and approval.

Line of Sight – A term to roughly define the effective distance of a radio operating on higher frequencies, where signals are not reflected by the ionosphere. Line of sight generally means that if the antennas of two stations are within visual range of each other, communications is possible. Intervening obstacles, mountains, valleys, buildings, etc. break the line of sight and may prevent communications.

LMR -- Land Mobile Radio

LTE -- Long Term Evolution is an enhancement to third generation 3G (third generation) wireless systems and is a follow-on to EDGE and HSPA. LTE does not meet all requirements of the 4G specification, but because it offers significant advances over earlier 3G data protocols, LTE is frequently marketed as a 4G system.

MAC –   Message Authentication Code

MARS –   (U.S.) Military Auxiliary Radio System

MEO -- Medium Earth Orbit is about 2,000 kilometers above the earth's surface.

MF –   Medium Frequency

Microcell – A low power cellular access point used to expand system coverage or penetrate into buildings with poor coverage. Sometimes called Femtocells, these units connect to an internet source and allow provide regular cell phone coverage. Microcell units should be obtained from wireless service providers to avoid interference issues.

Microwave – A nonspecific term usually used to refer to radio signals roughly in the 300 MHz to 300 GHz range, which is useful for point-to-point linking over a line of sight.

MiFi – A brand name, now often used generically, to describe a wireless router that provides a portable WiFi Hotspot.

MMR –   Maritime Mobile Radio

MOA –   Memorandum of Agreement

MotoTRBO – The Motorola application of digital mobile radio

MOU –   Memorandum of Understanding

Morse Code –   The radiotelegraph code developed by Samuel F.B. Morse became one of the world's principal languages for sending messages by using patterns of long and short pulses, first over telegraph wires and later over wireless systems. Currently, Morse Code is widely used as an unobtrusive station identification signal. Strictly speaking, the term *Morse Code* refers to the coding scheme itself, but in common use, it is taken to mean the process of communicating by long and short signals (dots and dashes) whether by audio, radio or flashing lights.

MSCA – Military Support to Civil Authorities. In the U.S., the term has been replaced by Defense Support of Civil Authorities, or DSCA)

MURS – Multi-Use Radio System

Mutual Aid Channel – A designated channel for agencies to communicate with outside responders assisting with a large or expanding event.

NAC – Network Access Code. NAC is a 12-bit code comprised of 3 Hex Digits, allowing 4026 unique addresses on the system.

Narrowband – Refers to the bandwidth of a radio transmission. As technology has permitted improvements in radio circuits, the FCC has progressively required most systems to transition to narrower bandwidths so that more users can access the spectrum.

NAWAS –   National Warning System

NCC –   (U.S.) Public Safety National Coordination Committee, a Federal Advisory Committee formed by the FCC to advise on interoperability issues.

NCC –   (U.S.) National Coordinating Center for Telecommunications.

NCS –   National Communications System

NIAR –   National Institute of Amateur Radio (India)

NIC –   NIMS Integration Center

NIFOG –   National Interoperability Field Operations Guide

NIMS –   National Incident Management System. In the U.S., NIMS provides a standard process for responding to and recovering from incidents at all levels and for all types of organizations.

NPSTC –   National Public Safety Telecommunications Council, a federation of organizations working to improve public safety communications and interoperability.

NOAA Weather Radio – See All-Hazards Radio.

Node – A point or address on a network, particularly one used for making connections.

NTIA – National Telecommunications and Information Administration

NTIA Manual – The NTIA Manual of Regulations and Procedures for Federal Radio Frequency Management.

NXDA – A two-way digital radio standard used in the U.S.

OSCAR – Orbital Satellite Carrying Amateur Radio

Outdoor Warning System – Loudspeakers or sirens used as an outdoor public warning and alerting system.

P25 – Project-25, often referred to as APCO-25. P25 is a commonly used radio interoperability standard in the U.S. for trunked public safety radio networks, but it is not used in all systems, as there are competing proprietary standards. An earlier protocol was known as P16. For several years, the FCC did not allow P25 signals on the amateur radio bands, but this restriction has been lifted for VHF, UHF and above.

Packet Radio – A standard digital mode for transmitting data by radio.

PACTOR – Packet Teleprinting Over Radio

PL Tone – A proprietary term for Continuous Tone-Coded Squelch System (CTCSS)

PPE – Personal Protective Equipment

PSAP – Public Service Answering Point

Public Safety Radio Service

RAID – Redundant Array of Independent Disks

Repeater – A radio set up to automatically relay radio signals, allowing greater distances to be covered by the system.

RF – Radio Frequency.

RF Hazard – The health and safety risk that is associated with being in proximity to radio frequency energy. There are published safety standards, based on power levels, frequency, and nature of exposure.

RJ-11 – Registered Jack-11 is a standard communications connector with two or four wires, commonly used for household telephones.

RoIP – Radio over Internet Protocol

RSGB – Radio Society of Great Britain

RTTY –   Radio Teletype

SAR –   Search and Rescue

SHARES –   Shared High Frequency Resources

SHF –   Super High Frequency

Shortwave – Generally refers to frequencies in the 1800 KHz to 30 MHz range. Radio signals in this range are capable of traveling thousands of miles.

Simplex – The process of sending and receiving sequentially. For voice systems, users take turns talking.

SITREP – Situation Report

Skype – A proprietary computer application that allows users to have video and audio calls.

Skywarn – In the U.S., a voluntary organization of trained weather observers that provide field reports to the National Weather Service. Skywarn observers do not "chase storms" in their Skywarn capacity, but rather observe and report from a safe distance.

Skywave – Radio signals that reflect off the ionosphere, allowing global radio communications. Normally these signals are in the frequency range of 1800 KHz to 30 MHz, although unusual ionospheric conditions can vary these numbers greatly.

SMS – Short Message Service, commonly provided by telephone, internet, and wireless providers.

SPOTREP – Spot Report, usually referring to an immediate report of important events directly from the field.

SSTV – Slow Scan Television

Switch – The mechanism within a switching or routing center that connects calls or routes circuits.

STA – Special Temporary Authority from the Federal Communications Commission, permitting temporary operation of a radio transmitter in a manner different from the authorization granted by the basic radio license.

T-1 – A legacy term for a data service or circuit providing the equivalent of 24 telephone calls. In Europe a similar service is called "E Carrier." Currently, the term is meant to be a data circuit providing 1.544 megabits per second.

T-3 – A legacy term for a data service or circuit that bundled 28 T-1 circuits. Currently the term refers to a data circuit providing 44.736 megabits per second.

Talkaround – In trunked radio systems, talkaround channels are similar to Simplex channels on a conventional system, and they allow limited communications in case of central system failure.

Talkgroup – In a trunked radio system, a Talkgroup is similar to a discreet channel on a conventional system. The talkgroup is a predefined group of stations, and when one user keys to transmit, the trunking system assigns a working frequency and signals all talkgroup radios to automatically listen to that frequency. In this way, a small number of actual radio frequencies may serve the needs of a large number of talkgroups.

TDMA –   Time Division Multiplex, one mode of digital radio transmission. TDMA is specified in the P25 interoperability standard.

Telco – Telephone Company

TELEX – A proprietary application of teletype, whereby a user could connect directly with another user's TELEX machine by dialing on a telephone-like device. FAX and Email largely eliminated TELEX in Europe and North America, but it is still in use in many developing countries.

Teletype – Essentially electric typewriters connected so that typing on one causes the distant one to type the same characters. Teletype can operate over wires or radio. The system originally used the Baudot code, which limited the character set to upper case letters, numbers, and a few common punctuation marks. Later systems use ASCII coding, which allows upper and lower case as well as virtually all symbols and marks. Teletype protocols are used in portable communications devices used by the deaf, and many public agencies have TTD (Teletype for the Deaf) devices.

TETRA –   European Terrestrial Trunked Radio, a major radio interoperability standard used throughout Europe. TETRA and P25 are not compatible.

Triangulation – The process of using radio direction finding techniques to locate the origin of a radio signal. Cell phone systems are able to use triangulationto determine the approximate location of a cell phone.

Trunking – Trunking radio systems use computers to dynamically configure a limited number of frequencies into working Talkgroups on demand, essentially setting up temporary radio networks on demand.

Twisted Pair – A term to describe regular telephone wiring, which is essentially two insulated wires twisted together.

Twitter – A proprietary short message service that provides 140-character messages, widely used as a social media communications tool.

TTY – Teletype. Variations on the term are RTTY (Radio Teletype) and TTD (Teletype for the Deaf).

VHF – Very High Frequency

Vocoder – Voice Encoder, generally referring to the module which converts analog voice into digital signals.

VoIP – Voice over Internet Protocol

VPN – Virtual Private Network

VSAT – Very Small Aperture Terminal, generally in reference to a two-way satellite dish antenna that is less than three meters in diameter. In practice, VSAT dish antennas are usually 0.75 to 1.5 meters in diameter.

UAV – Unmanned Aerial Vehicle

UHF – Ultra High Frequency

VPC – VHF Public Coast Area

Wavelength – Electromagnetic waves, including radio, can be characterized by frequency or wavelength. Knowing the wavelength is necessary in order to devise efficient antennas. The higher the frequency, the shorter the wavelength.

WEA – Wireless Emergency Alert

WebEOC® – Web-based Emergency Operations Center

WINLINK -- A wireless email system used by amateur radio operators, MARS, many private sailors and others. WINLINK allows remote stations to send and receive regular emails, on HF, VHF or UHF, as needed, through a worldwide system of gateway stations and mail servers.

WIRES® – Wide-Coverage Internet Repeater Enhancement System links radio repeaters around the world, allowing users with Yaesu and compatible analog radios world-wide coverage.

WISP – Wireless Internet Service Provider.

WPS – Wireless Priority Service, a program of the U.S. Department of Homeland Security, allows designated wireless phones to receive priority access for calling.

WL2K – WinLink 2000, a wireless messaging system that exchanges email between users in the field and any email address and which can be used to bypass failed internet segments. WL2K is widely used by MARS, recreational sailors and amateur radio operators.

International Issues

Radio licensing is at the prerogative of national governments. Even within the European Union, where national standards are generally coordinated, there are significant differences in policies and procedures among countries regarding licensing and privileges.

It is usually a serious criminal offense to operate a radio transmitter (and sometimes even a receiver) without the appropriate license from the national authority. In some cases, this applies even to devices that many users consider to be unregulated, such as satellite phones and low power two-way radios and wireless headsets.

Amateur radio international operations have been somewhat simplified by several programs such as reciprocal licensing, and treaties such as the CEPT agreement, which allows for automatic authority for European, U.S., Canadian, and many British Commonwealth hams, traveling in signatory countries. In some cases, this includes the semi-autonomous overseas territories of the signatory country and in other cases it does not. The following graphic shows the general availability of foreign operating privileges on the amateur radio bands:

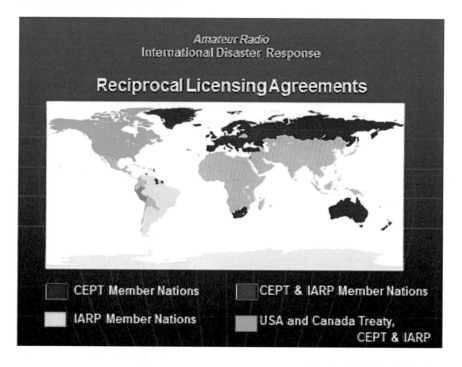

USA-Specific Issues

The Federal Emergency Management Agency (FEMA) has extensive resources available to state, territorial, tribal and local governments during communications emergencies.

Managed through the Response Directorate, the resources of the FEMA Disaster Emergency Communications function and Mobile Emergency Response Support detachments, may be available upon request of states, tribes, and territories.

For further information, contact the Regional Emergency Communications Coordinator at your servicing FEMA Regional Headquarters.

In addition, each region of the U.S. is supported by a Regional Emergency Communications Coordination Working Group (RECCWG), supported by the FEMA Regional Emergency Communications Coordinator. The RECCWG is comprised of members from all levels of government, industry and relevant NGOs.

In July 2014, the Federal Emergency Management Agency and the ARRL, the national association for amateur radio, implemented a Memorandum of Agreement outlining cooperation and coordination in emergency communications.

Federally-recognized Tribal Governments are entitled to request a Presidential Disaster Declaration and emergency communications assistance directly from the federal government through FEMA. Recent amendments to the Stafford Act provide the process through which Tribal Governments may exercise this authority.

Photo Courtesy of the Chickasaw Nation and FEMA

U.S. Radio Frequency Allocation Table

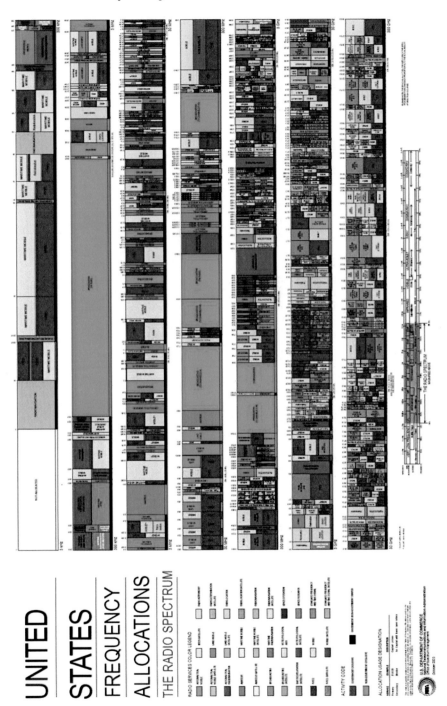

Appendices

Field Operations Guides

The DHS Office of Emergency Communications publishes two extremely helpful Field Operations Guides, which are available for download at no cost. A limited number of printed copies may be available, but as a rule, users should plan to print their own copies. The documents are:

National Interoperability Field Operations Guide (NIFOG)

http://www.safecomprogram.gov/nifog.html

Auxiliary Interoperability Field Operations Guide (AUXFOG)

http://www.publicsafetytools.info/auxfog/start_auxfog_info.php

Amateur Radio Public Service Communications Manual

http://www.arrl.org/public-service-communications-manual

Bibliography

Background Information
- --, "A Guide for Applying Information Technology in Law Enforcement," National Law Enforcement and Corrections Technology Center, NCJ 185934, March 2001.
- --, Final Report of the Public Safety Wireless Advisory Committee to the Federal Communications Commission and the National Telecommunications And Information Administration, 11 September 1996.
- --, "Integrated Justice Information Systems – The Department of Justice Initiative," 12 April 2000.
- --, MobileIN.com, "Public Safety and Homeland Security."
- --, "The State of Public Safety Communications," SAFECOM presentation at Internat'l Symp. on Advanced Radio Technologies, 2 March 2004.
- --, "Statement of Requirements for Public Safety Wireless Communications and Interoperability" (version 1.1, 2006), The SAFECOM Program, US Dept. of Homeland Security, version 1.1, 27 October 2005.
- Remarks by DHS Secretary Chertoff at the Tactical Interoperable Communications Conference, 5/8/06.
- C. Doyle, "A Roadmap for Integrating Modeling and Simulation for Emergency Response," NIST Simulation Conference, March 2004.
- R. I. Desourdis, et al., *Emerging Public Safety Wireless Communication Systems*. Boston – Artech House, 2002.
- A. A. Fatah, J. A. Barrett, R. D. Arcilesi, P. A. Scolla, C. H. Lattin, and S. D. Fortner, "Guide for the Selection of Communication Equipment for Emergency First Responders," National Institute of Justice Guide 104-00, February 2002.
- K. J. Imel and J. W. Hart, "Understanding Wireless Communications in Public Safety" (Second Edition), National Law Enforcement and Corrections Technology Center, January 2003.
- D. Lum, "You Say You Want an Evolution?" *Radio Resource International*, Q1 2006. Also published in an extended version, entitled "Introduction to Government Radio Systems."
- J. R. McMillian Jr., *The Primer of Public Safety Telecommunication Systems*, 3rd ed. Daytona Beach, FL – APCO International, 2000.
- M. J. Taylor, R. C. Epper, and T. Tolman, "State and Local Law Enforcement Wireless Communications and Interoperability – A Quantitative Analysis," NCJ 168961, January 1998.
- A. Theil and H. Stambaugh, "Improving Firefighter Communications," FEMA report tr-099.

Commercial Wireless Services

- --, "An Overview of the SMR Service from the Perspective of Public Safety," PSWN Report, 2001.
- --, "Commercial Wireless Applicability Report," PSWN, May 2000.
- --, "Commercial Wireless Technologies for Public Safety Users," Center for Criminal Justice Technology, July 2000.
- --, "Data-Optimized Wireless Technology," Qualcomm web pages on 1xEV-DO.
- S. Buckingham, "What Is General Packet Radio Service?" GSM World web pages.
- Y.-M. Chuang, et al., "Trading CDPD Availability and Voice Blocking Probability in Cellular Networks," *IEEE Network*, March/April 1998, pp. 48-52.
- J. Duffy, "Wireless Data Service Options Explode," *Network World Fusion*, 19 April 2004.
- E. Edenholm, "Cellular Digital Packet Data Helps Improve Efficiency," APCO Bulletin, November 1996.
- T. Fujiwara, et al., "A Wireless Network Scheme Enhanced with Ad-Hoc Networking for Emergency Communications," Wireless and Optical Comm. (WOC'03), Banff, Canada, July 14-16, 2003.
- I. S. Ghai and A. Johnston, "Wireless LAN IP Phones-Simplifying Communications?" *New Telephony*, 29 April 2004.
- J. Jackson, "Colorado City Switches Protocols to Keep Vehicles on Track," *Government Computer News*, 2 August 2004.
- C. Kain, "Commercial Mobile Radio Services for Public Sector Agencies," Mitretek Systems, Inc., prepared for the USDOT ITS Joint Program Office, October 2003.
- K. Kenedy, "Sprint PCS Offers Wireless Service as CDPD Replacement Option," *CRN*, 29 October 2003.
- J. Kobielus, "SMS pushes paging to extinction," *Network World Fusion*, 7 January 2002.
- S. Lawson, "ATT to shut down CDPD wireless network," ITWorld.com, 29 October 2002.
- L. Luna, "Heavens Help Us" [satellite communication systems], *Mobile Radio Technology*, August 2005.
- D. Robb, "The Cellular Option − Cellular PC Cards Give You Another Choice for Wireless Data Transmission," *Government Computer News*, 8 September 2003.
- A. Rosenberg, "Instant Voice Messaging (IVM) in the Enterprise; IVM, or Push-to-Talk, is all about the convergence of traditional half-duplex radio walkie-talkies with VoIP-based wireless phones," CommWeb, 24 February 2003.
- R. Rybicki, "Cellular Digital Packet Data in Michigan Law Enforcement," APCO Bulletin, September 1996.
- E. Schwartz, "CDPD premortem," *InfoWorld*, 11 April 2003.

- E. Schwartz, "Old CDPD network causing new problems," *InfoWorld*, 7 April 2003
- B. Smith, "Police grapple with CDPD roadblock," *Wireless Week*, 18 November 2002.
- B. Smith, "Police Drive Into Next Gen," *Wireless Week*, 1 August 2003.

M. S. Taylor, et al., *Internet Mobility – the CDPD Approach*. New York – Prentice-Hall, 1996.

Emergency Communications
- APCO International, *What Telecommunicators Should Know about Spectrum,* Association of Public Safety Communications Officials, www.apco.org
- ARRL, *Amateur Radio Public Service Handbook,* Publication Number 4845, www.arrl.org/shop
- ARRL, *Emergency Power,* Publication Number 6153.
- ARRL, *Field Resources Manual*, Publication Number 5439.
- ARRL, *Introduction to Emergency Communications Course Book,* Publication Number 7303, www.arrl.org/shop
- ARRL, *Storm Spotting and Amateur Radio*, Pub. Number 0908.
- P.A. Erickson, *Emergency Response Planning for Corporate and Municipal Managers*, Academic Press.
- ICMA, *Telecommunications for Local Government*, International City Manager's Association Practical Management Series. www.icma.org
- Alan M. Levitt, *Disaster Planning and Recovery, A Guide for Facility Professionals,* John Wiley and Sons, 1997.
- SIA, *First Responder's Guide to Satellite Communications,* Satellite Industry Association, www.sia.org
- Stanford H. Rowe, II, *Business Telecommunications,* Maxwell Macmillan International.
- Leo A. Wrobel, *Disaster Recovery Planning for Telecommunications,* Artech House, Boston.

History of Telecommunications
- --, FCC web pages on refarming history
- --, "One-way Police Radio Communication," IEEE History Center.
- --, "The Power That Made Radio Realistic," FCC History web page
- P. B. Petersen, "The First Two-Way Police Radio Systems," Infoage library of broadcasts.
- T. H. White, "Early Government Regulation (1903-1946)," section 23 of Early United States Radio History.

Incident Command Communications

- --, National Incident Management System, US Department of Homeland Security, 1 March 2004.
- --, "NYU Researchers Work with NYC Fire Department," Firehouse.com, 2 February 2004.
- P. J. Camp, et al., "Supporting Communication and Collaboration Practices in Safety-Critical Situations," *Proc. Human Factors in Computing Systems* (CHI 2000). The Hague, Netherlands.
- M. Douglas, "Incident Management in Many Forms," *Mobile Radio Technology*, July 2004.
- S. Lewis, Firefighter Communication System Project Description, Georgia Tech, 1999.
- S. P. McGrath, et al., "ARTEMIS − A Vision for Remote Triage and Emergency Management Information Integration," Darmouth University.
- C. Varone, "Command's Right Hand − Part 1," *Fire Chief*, 1 March 2000.
- X. Jiang, et al., "Ubiquitous Computing for Firefighters − Field Studies and Prototypes of Large Displays for Incident Commanders," 2004 Conf. on Human Factors in Computing Systems (CHI 2004).

Interoperability

- --, "A Cooperative Systems Architecture for Interoperability," EADS white paper.
- --, "Can We Talk? Public Safety and the Interoperability Challenge," *NIJ Journal*, April 2000.
- --, "Guide to Radio Communications Interoperability Strategies and Products," AGILE Report TE-02-02, NLECTC-NE (Rome, NY), 1 April 2003.
- --, "Minneapolis Post-Symposium Report," PSWN document, July 2001.
- --, "Now − a cost-effective solution for high-level emergency interoperability," M/A-COM *Channels*, vol. 3, issue 1.
- --, "Operational Test Bed-Alexandria (OTB-A) Communications Interoperability Gateway Subsystem Operational Test Document, AGILE Report TE-00-04, NLECTC-NE (Rome, NY), 23 July 2001.
- --, "Statewide Communication Interoperability Planning (SCIP) Methodology," SAFECOM program, 1 November 2004.
- --, "Summit on Interoperable Communications for Public Safety," 26-27 June 2003.
- --, "When They Can't Talk, Lives Are Lost," NTFI brochure.
- --, "Why Can't We Talk − Working Together to Bridge the Communications Gap to Save Lives," NTFI publication.
- -- "Technical Evaluation of the TRP-1000 and ACU-1000--Test Procedures and Results," AGILE Document No. TE-00-0002-01," AGILE project memo, 15 June 2001.

- A. Emondi, "Communications Interoperability for Public Safety and Law Enforcement Agencies," presentation at IACP 27th Annual LEIM Training Conference, May 2003.
- M. Hachman, "PacketHop Wireless Mesh Network Survives Initial Trial," *eWeek*, 25 February 2004.
- G. Hobar, "First Responders and Interoperability," presentation at SUPERCOMM 2003.
- T. Hoyne, "Intercommunications-Achieving Interoperability Through IP," *9-1-1 Magazine*, July/August 2002.
- A. Joch, "Communications Breakdown," *Federal Computer Week*, 5 December 2005.
- J. Lin, "Philadelphia Mayday Calls – Heard or Not?" Firehouse.com, 30 September 2004.
- V. Mayer-Schonberger, "Emergency Communications – the Quest for Interoperability in the United States and Europe," Discussion Paper 2002-7, John F. Kennedy School of Government, Harvard University, March 2002.
- W. Pessimier, "Top Priority – A Fire Service Guide to Interoperable Communications" (IAFC Interoperability Handbook), 2005.
- D. Sarkar, "Fixing a Communications Breakdown," *Federal Computer Week*, 22 July 2002.
- R. Schoen, "Interoperable Communications – Is Mesh Technology the Answer?" PFI
- D. Siegle and R. Murphy, "Interoperability Report Card – PSWN Grades the Progress," *Mobile Radio Technology*, 1 June 2001.
- D. Storey, "Digital Two-Way Radios Address Interoperability Dilemma," *Government Procurement*, June 2004.
- M. J. Taylor, et al., "Wireless Communication and Interoperability Among State and Local Law Enforcement Agencies," National Institute of Justice Research in Brief, January 1998.

Location and Location-Based Services

- "Automatic Vehicle Location System," of King County, WA
- "Automatic Vehicle Location Systems Explained," Air-Trak
- U. Toronto, web resources on GIS theory
- "Location in Demand – A Look at Wireless Location and the Need for Versatility, Value and Demand," True Position white paper.
- M. D. Adickes, et al., "Optimization Of Indoor Wireless Communication Network Layouts," *IIE Transactions*, Vol. 34, pp. 823-836, 2002.
- R. Allan, "OnStar System Puts Telematics on the Map," *Electronic Design*, 31 March 2003.
- C. Biever, "Wi-Fi Finds the Way When GPS Can't," *New Scientist*, 28 June 2004.
- S. Blacksher and T. Foley, "Boulder HOPS Aboard GPS Tracking," *GPS World*, 1 January 2002.

- J. Blyer, "Location-Based Services Are Positioned for Growth," *Wireless Systems Design*, September 2003, pp. 16-20.
- J. J. Caffery and G. L. Stuber, "Overview of radiolocation in CDMA cellular systems," *IEEE Communications Magazine*, April 1998, pp. 38-45.
- N. Davies et al., "Using and Determining Location in a Context-Sensitive Tour Guide," *IEEE Computer Magazine*, August 2001, pp. 35-41.
- G. M. Djuknik and R. E. Richton, "Geolocation and Assisted GPS," Lucent Technologies white paper.
- M. Feuerstein, "The Complex World of Wireless E911," *Mobile Radio Technology*, August 2004.
- W. B. Howard, "From AVL to MRM," *Mission Critical Communications*, November-December 2005.
- D. Jackson, "Not Just for Trucks Anymore" [AVL], *Mobile Radio Technology*, 1 June 2003.
- X. Jiang, et al., "Siren – Context-Aware Computing for Firefighters," *Proc. 2004 Pervasive Computing Conference*, Vienna.
- M. Korkea-aho, "Context-Aware Applications Survey," Helsinki University of Technology report, April 2000.
- K. Lorincz and M. Welsh, "A Robust, Decentralized Approach to RF-Based Location Tracking," Technical Report TR-19-04, Harvard University, 2004.
- L. E. Miller, "Indoor Navigation for First Responders – A Feasibility Study," NIST project report, February 2006. (5.7 MB pdf)
- D. Sarkar, "Florida Firefighters Test Geolocation," *Federal Computer Week*, 22 August 2003.
- K. Taylor, "Busted by GPS/AVL," *Mobile Radio Technology*, May 2001.
- Y. Zhao, "Standardization of Mobile Phone Positioning for 3G Systems," *IEEE Communications Magazine*, July 2002, pp. 108-116.

Miscellaneous

- --, "Informational Material – 'How To' Guide for Establishing and Managing Talk Groups," PSWN document, October 2001.
- --, Summary of National Fire Service Research Agenda Symposium, Emmitsburg, MD, June 1-3, 2005.
- N. Baisa, "Designing Wireless Interfaces for Patient Monitoring Equipment," *RF Design*, April 2005.
- B. Cash, "5.9 GHz Dedicated Short Range Communication (DSRC) Overview," ARINC Inc. presentation, December 2002.
- J. Darlington, "In-Building the Perfect System" [BDA installation], *Mission Critical Communications*, April 2006.
- R. D'Avello and J. Van Bosch, "Portable and Embedded Wireless Devices as Conduit for Telematics Applications," *Proc. Convergence 2002*. Reprinted in *IEEE Vehicular Technology Soc. News*, February 2004, pp. 14-24.
- T. Dees, "Information and Communications Technology for Public Safety," IQ Service report to International City/Council Management Association, January 2000.
- M. DiCristofano, "Wireless Use Helps to Meet Public Safety Budget Limits," *Mobile Radio Technology*, 1 August 1997.
- D. Grip, "A Group Effort – Public Safety Consortiums Help Small-Town Agencies Deploy Wireless Technology," *APCO Bulletin*, August 2000.
- D. N. Hatfield, "Technological Trends for Wireless Communications," Report to Gallaudet University, 11 July 1997.
- D. Jackson, "PacketHop Spawns Mesh Networking," *Mobile Radio Technology*, August 2004.
- J. Jackson, "Keeping Digital Tabs on Kids in an Emergency," *Government Computer News*, 12 July 2004.
- W. Jackson, "First Responders in a Jam?" *Government Computer News*, 15 May 2006.
- W. W. Jones, et al., "Workshop to Define Information Needed by Emergency Responders during Building Emergencies," NISTIR 7193, January 2005.
- J. Kumagi and S. Cherry, "Sensors and Sensibility," *IEEE Spectrum*, July 2004, pp. 22-28.
- T. Lane, "Radio-Over-IP," *Mission Critical Communications*, August 2004, pp. 34-41.
- D. Oaks, "Fight or Flight?" [wildfires] *Fire Chief Magazine*, 1 April 2000.
- J. A. Ochoa et al., "Advanced Law Enforcement Vehicle Electronics and Associated Power," *Proc. 1999 IEEE Digital Avionics Systems Conf.*, paper 8.B.6.
- D. Sarkar, "SAFECOM Absorbs Public Safety Network," FCW.com, 15 January 2004.

- C. Werner, "Communications — The Katrina Effect," Firehouse.com, 29 September 2005.
- C. Werner, "Public Safety's Conundrum," *Mobile Radio Technology*, February 2006.

Mobile Data Applications
- "Bringing Wireless Data Applications to the Patrol Car," PSWN Program Information Brief 0401, February 2001.
- "Why Wireless for Public Safety?" page on Wireless Ready.
- M. Angell, "Police Departments Upgrading Their Mobile Wireless Networks," *Investor's Business Daily*, 17 March 2004.
- D. Bishop, "Mobile Data Ideas Grow in 'Greenhouse Project'," MRT , 29 August 2001.
- B. Bruegge and B. Bennington, "Applications of wireless research to real industrial problems. Applications of mobile computing and communication," *IEEE Personal Communications*, February 1996, pp. 64-71.
- A. Burnett, "The Evolution of Mobile Data," *Mission Critical Communications*, May 2005, pp. 78-80.
- B. Charney, "Helping cops keep tabs on wireless data," CNET News.com, 17 March 2003.
- D. Frank, "Montana Puts Vehicle Data ," FCW.com, 26 February 2004.
- C. Greenman, "A Well-Equipped Patrol Officer — Gun, Flashlight, Computer," *New York Times*, 21 January 1999.
- H. Havenstein, "Building for Mobility — Handheld App Developers Aim for Harmony with the Enterprise," *Federal Computer Week*, 26 May 2003.
- D. A. Keckler, "The Future of Fire Mobile Data," *Mobile Radio Technology*, 1 August, 1999.
- I. Ramirez and R. Coffey, "Enhancing Law Enforcement Efficiency with Mobile Data — The Wireless Interoperability Advantage," *9-1-1 Magazine*, July/August 2002.
- S. Ring, "Mobile Digital Communication for Public Safety, Law Enforcement, and Non-Tactical Military," ETSI document, Jan. 2001.
- D. Sarkar, "Mobile Units Aid Small City in Big Way," *Federal Computer Week*, 20 February 2004.

Networking Technology Assessments
- --, "Meeting 21st Century Public Safety Challenges Today," Cisco Systems white paper, 2003.
- --, Cisco Corp., "Voice-over-IP Overview."
- B. Bouwers, "TETRA Over IP," TETRA World Congress 2003 Workshop presentation.
- H. Cheung, "Data Services and Applications Including IP," TETRA World Congress 2003 Workshop presentation.

- J. Davidson and J. Peters, "Overview of the PSTN and Comparison to Voice Over IP," Chapter 1 of *Voice Over IP Fundamentals*. Cisco Press, 2001.
- M. Douglas, "IP on the Rise," *First Responder Communications* supplement to *Mobile Radio Technology*, August 2004.
- M. Douglas, "Pocket Policing," *Mobile Radio Technology*, 1 May 2003.
- J. Ellis, "The Next Phase, Applications Using the Converged Network," Chapter 14 of *Voice, Video and Data Network Convergence*. New York – Elsevier, 2003.
- H. Fiderer, "IP at the PSAP," Public Safety Report supplement to *Mission Critical Communications*, November-December 2005.
- I. Guardini, et al., "The Role of Internet Technology in Future Mobile Data Systems," *IEEE Communications Magazine*, November 2000, pp. 68-72.
- T. A. Hall, "Objective Speech Quality Measures for Internet Telephony," *Proceedings of the SPIE*, vol. 4522 – Voice Over IP (VoIP) Technology.
- R. Hixson, "IP and E9-1-1," *Mission Critical Communications*, June 2004, pp. 78-79.
- D. Jackson, "Texas City Decides to Mesh Around," *Mobile Radio Technology*, February 2004.
- J. Jackson, "DARPA Takes Aim at IT Sacred Cows," *Government Computer News*, 11 March 2004.
- W. Jackson, "VOIP lets 911 callers down, communications officials say," *Government Computer News*, 11 December 2003.
- K. Lorincz, et al., "Sensor Networks for Emergency Response – Challenges and Opportunities," *IEEE Pervasive Computing*, Oct.-Dec. 2004, pp. 16-23.
- R. Merritt, "DARPA Looks Past Ethernet, IP Nets," *EE Times*, 26 April 2004.
- R. Merritt, "Mesh Network Wireless Spec Contemplated," *EE Times*, 8 December 2003.
- K. Middaugh, "No More Towers," *Government Technology*, May 2004.
- M. Rauf and F. Lefebvre, "Keeping the Wireless Connection Running," *E-9-1-1 Magazine*, January/ February 2003.
- S. Riesen, "The Usage of Mainstream Technologies for Public Safety and Security Networks," Helsinki Univ. of Technology, master's thesis, 9 October 2003.
- D. S. Sharp, et al., "Analysis of Public Safety Traffic on Trunked Land Mobile Radio Systems," *IEEE J. Sel. Areas in Comm.*, vol. 22, pp. 1197-1205 (September 2004); errata, *IEEE J. Sel. Areas in Comm.*, vol. 23, p. 186 (January 2005).
- E. Sutherland, "Wireless As a Tool for Improving Public Safety," Wireless IM ().

- A. Thiessen, "Public Safety Digital Communications Advancement in Mobile Ad Hoc Networking," presentation at AGILE program review, July 2003.

Radio Technology Assessments
- --, "Comparisons of Conventional and Trunked Systems," Public Safety Wireless Network, May 1999.
- --, Commercial Wireless Performance Evaluation Comparison & Applicability Report, SAFECOM document, June 1999.
- --, "EDACS Explained," ComNet Ericsson white paper.
- --, "How-To Guide for Managing the Radio System Life Cycle," PSWN systems planning resource, 2002.
- --, "Michigan Approves Upgrade to Statewide Public Safety, Public Service Radio System," Motorola press release, 12 November 2001.
- --, "Public Safety Land Mobile Radio Systems – A Roadmap for Systems Development," PSWN systems planning resource, 2002.
- --, "Technology Independent Methodology for the Modeling, Simulation, and Empirical Verification of Wireless Communication System Performance in Noise and Interference Limited Systems Operating on Frequencies Between 30 and 1500 MHz," TIA TR8 Report WG88-20, May 1997.
- J. Ashley, "Trunking the EDACS Way," *Mobile Radio Technology*, 1 February 1999.
- P. Frazier, et al., "Current Status, Knowledge Gaps, and Research Needs Pertaining to Firefighter Radio Communication Systems," TriData Corp. report to NIOSH, September 2003.
- R. Isbell, "Up and Out in Pennsylvania," *Mobile Radio Technology*, 1 February 2000.
- E. Jacobsen, "A Brief Examination of CQPSK for CPE PHY Modulation," IEEE 802.16 document pc-00/11.
- A. Joch, "Digital Radios – A New Calling Plan," *Federal Computer Week*, 21 June 2004.
- J. Jones, "Reach for the Sky – South Dakota Proves That Big Dreams Can Lead to Big Successes" [about SD radio system], *Federal Computer Week*, 30 August 2004.
- L. Luna, "Push-to-Talk," *Mobile Radio Technology*, 1 April 2003.
- R. J. Matheson, "A Survey of Relative Spectrum Efficiency of Mobile Voice Communication Systems," NTIA Report 94-311, July 1994.
- D. Mohney, "Fighting Over the Future of P25," *Mobile Radio Technology*, June 2005.
- C. D. Moore, "Projecting the Technological Evolution of the Private Land Mobile Radio Services," *Proc. IEEE Vehicular Technology Conf.*, May 1989, pp. 38-43.
- Motorola, Inc., "Scalable Adaptive Modulation (SAM) Physical Layer Technology," presentation, 2001.

- A. Seybold, "Commercial PTT Falls Short in Mission-Critical Setting," *Mission Critical Communications*, July 2004, p. 156.
- W. C. Stone, "NIST Construction Automation Report No. 3 – Electromagnetic Signal Attenuation in Construction Materials," October 1997.
- M. D. Wade, "Cellular and Trunking in Disaster Areas," APCO Bulletin, May 1998.
- M. Worrell and A. MacFarlane, "Phoenix Fire Department Radio System Safety Project Final Report," October 2004.

Regulation and Spectrum
- --, "FCC Adopts Solution to Interference Problem Faced by 800 MHz Public Safety Radio Systems," FCC news release, 8 July 2004.
- --, FCC Docket 03-108, "Notice of Proposed Rule Making and Order In the Matter of Facilitating Opportunities for Flexible, Efficient, and Reliable Spectrum Use Employing Cognitive Radio Technologies Authorization and Use of Software Defined Radios," December 2003.
- --, "FCC Issues Narrowband Mandate Below 512 MHz," APCO news release, February 2003.
- --, FCC Second Report and Order and Further Notice of Proposed Rulemaking in the matter of the 4.9 GHz Band Transferred from Federal Use, 27 February 2002.
- --, FCC Ruling in the Matter of the Transfer of 4.9 GHz from Government Use, 2 May 2003.
- --, FCC Memorandum Opinion and Order 96-492.
- --, FCC Notice of Proposed Rulemaking In the Matter of Improving Public Safety Communications in the 800 MHz Band and Consolidating the 900 MHz Industrial/Land Transportation and Business Pool Channels, 15 March 2002.
- --, FCC Report to Congress on the Study to Assess Short-Term and Long-Term Needs for Allocations of Additional Portions of the Electromagnetic Spectrum for Federal, State and Local Emergency Response Providers, 19 December 2005.
- --, FCC Spectrum Policy Task Force Report, November 2002.
- --, Minutes of the Twentieth and Final Meeting of the Public Safety National Coordination Committee, 17 July 2003.
- --, "Refarming – Truths and Myths," Tyco-M/A COM white paper.
- --, Report of the FCC Spectrum Efficiency Working Group, November 2002.
- J. Careless, "Speak Easy – Technologies to Improve Two-Way Communications for First Responders," *Frontline First Responder*, June 2002.
- T. L. Chirhart, et al., "Alternative Frequencies for Use by Public Safety Systems," NTIA report 01-48.
- J. P. Camacho, et al., "US National Spectrum Requirements – Projections and Trends," NTIA Spectrum Engineering Report 94-31.

- P. J. Daronco, et al., "Alternative Frequencies for Use by Public Safety Systems," FCC report, 18 January 2002.
- A. Davidson and L. Marturano, "The Impact of Digital Technologies on Future Land Mobile Spectrum Requirements," *Proc. IEEE Vehicular Technology Conf.*, May 1993, pp. 560-563.
- M. Greczyn, "Public Safety Leaders Stress Key Spectrum Needs After September 11," *Communications Daily*, November 19, 2001.
- P. Mannion, "Sharing Spectrum the Smarter Way," *EE Times*, 5 April 2004, pp. 18-20.
- P. Mannion, "Va. Tech Finds Soft Radio's Missing Link," *EE Times*, 16 August 2004.
- J. Powell, "Cognitive and Software Radio – A Public Safety Regulatory Perspective," report to NPSTC meeting, June 2004.
- B. Webb, "Report on FCC Docket 99-87 – RF Spectrum Refarming and FCC Mandated Requirements for Narrowband Migration," State of Utah Information Technology Services report, 18 January 2004.

Standards

- --, "Digital Public Safety Radio Communications – The Wireless Industry to the Rescue," TIA Industry Update Session at SUPERCOMM 2003.
- --, Project 25/34 New Technology Standards Project Statement of Requirements – Wideband Aeronautical and Terrestrial Mobile Digital Radio Technology Standards For the Wireless Transport of Rate Intensive Information, June 1, 1999.
- --, Project 25 Standards for Public Safety Digital Radio, December 2002.
- --, Project MESA "Service Specification Group Services and Applications, Statement of Requirements."
- O. Arrhenius, "Overview of TETRA and its Services and Facilities," TETRA World Congress 2003 Workshop presentation.
- S. Bartlett, "Does the digital radio standard come up short?" *Mobile Radio Technology*, 1 April 2001.
- W. Leland, "TR-8 – Mobile and Personal Private Radio Standards," presentation at SUPERCOMM 2003.
- L. Luna, "Project MESA Reaches a Crossroad," *MRT First Responder Communications*, April 2006.
- H. McEwen, "Voice Over Internet Protocol – The Implications for Public Safety," *Police Chief*, April 2005.
- M. Metcalf, "Project MESA – Advanced Mobile Broadband Communications for Public Safety Applications," *Proc. 2003 IEEE Personal, Indoor, and Mobile Radio Conf.*, Beijing, China, September 2003.
- B. Olson, "P25 Debate – The Digital Standard Revisited," *Mobile Radio Technology*, July 2001.

- D. Pfohl, et al., "The Importance of the Project 25 Common Air Interface and Its Potential Impact on Interoperability," APCO Bulletin, May 1999.
- S. Ring, "Mobile Digital Communication for Public Safety, Law Enforcement, and Non-Tactical Military," ETSI document.
- S. Tucker, et al., "The Technologies, Applications and Attributes of a Project 25 Trunking System," APCO Bulletin, May 1999.

Wideband/Broadband for Public Safety
- --, "CALPHOTO Portal Allows Investigators to Query Photo Archives Throughout the State," Microsoft case studies.
- --, "Medford, Oregon Deploys City-Wide Mobile Broadband Network from Meshnetworks," MeshNetworks press release, 23 February 2004.
- --, "NexGen City Produces Industry's First Push-To-Talk Handheld Communicator for Mesh-Based Public Safety Broadband Networks," NexGen City news release, 4 May 2004.
- --, Report of the Defense Science Board Task Force on Wideband Radio Frequency Modulation – Dynamic Access to Mobile Information Networks, July 2003.
- B. Brewin, "NYC Wireless Network Will Be Unprecedented," *Computer World*, 21 June 2004.
- M. Greczyn, "NCC Panels Look to Wideband Data for Public Safety at 700 MHz," *Communications Daily*, November 2001.
- B. Grimes, "Wireless Gets Connected – Cities Eye Mesh Networks for Market Communications," *Washington Technology*, 26 January 2004.
- C. Hoymann, et al., "Performance Analysis of TETRA and TAPS and Implications for Future Broadband Public Safety Communication Systems," Internationall Workshop on Broadband Wireless Ad-Hoc Networks and Services, September 2002.
- D. Jackson, "Emissions Mask for 4.9 GHz Under Fire," *First Responder Communications* supplement to MRT, August 2004.
- D. Jackson, "Panel – 4.9GHz Band Promising, Challenging," *Mobile Radio Technology*, 30 March 2004.
- W. Jackson, "Slice of the Spectrum – DC's Fledgling Network for First Responders Underscores the Bandwidth Battles," *Government Computer News*, 2 August 2004.
- L. Luna, "4.9 GHz Networks More Secure, But a Long Way Off," *Mobile Radio Technology*, 1 January 2004.
- E. B. Parizo, "Wireless Experts Call for an IP Overhaul," SearchMobileComputing.com, 23 March 2004.
- B. Robinson, "More Planned for Oregon Wireless System," *Federal Computer Week*, 3 March 2004.

Wireless LAN Applications

- --, "Syracuse Police Dept. Extends its WLAN to Field Officers," *Mobile Village* (), 8 September 2003.
- --, "Vytek and Symbol Technologies Provide Los Angeles Police Department with Innovative Handheld Computing Public Safety Solution," Symbol Technologies Press Release.
- --, "Wi-Fi with a PS Twist," APCO Bulletin article.
- J. Barthold, "Small-town Police Force Thinks Big," *Mobile Radio Technology*, 1 April 2004, p.6.
- N. Borisov, et al., "Intercepting Mobile Communications − The Insecurity of 802.11," *Proc. Mobicom 2003*.
- J. Careless, "Public Safety Applications for 802.11b," *Mobile Radio Technology*, 1 April 2002.
- M. V. Clark, et al., "Outdoor IEEE 802.11 Cellular Networks − Radio Link Performance," *Proc. 2002 IEEE Internat'l Comm. Conf.*, paper B13-1.
- J. P. Craiger, "802.11, 802.1X, and Wireless Security," 23 June 2002.
- P. DeBeasi, "Wireless LAN Security Protocols," *Wireless Design and Development*, April 2004, pp. 42-48.
- D. Knuth, "802.11b − Wireless LAN in Public Safety," Northrop Grumman brochure.
- J. Rendon, "Notebooks and Wi-Fi Keep Colorado Cops on the Beat," SearchMobile.com, 8 March 2004.
- P. Scanlon, "PDAs in the Field," presentation at IACP 27th Annual LEIM Training Conference, May 2003.
- T. Walsh, "Colorado City Gases Up WiFi Hot Spots," *Government Computer News*, 19 December 2003.

Index

911 Center, 29

Acknowledgements, iii

Amateur Radio Auxiliary Communications, 99

Amateur Radio Emergency Service, 45, 72, 76, 85, 100, 112

Amateur radio international operations, 127

Amateur Radio Public Service Communications Manual, 133

Amateur Radio Service, 111

APCO International, 137

ARES, 36, 45, 72, 76, 78, 85, 112

ARRL, 112, 128, 137

AUXFOG, 133

Auxiliary Communications, 45, 46, 72, 99

Background Information, 135

Backup Communications Systems, 43, 44

Baseline Needs Assessment, 19

Basic Considerations, 17

Bibliography, 135

Built-In Redundancy, 70

Canadian Coast Guard Auxiliary, 98

CAP, 97

Capability, 17

Capability Needs Assessment, 57

Civil Air Patrol, 72, 97

civil aviation disaster, 5

Coast Guard Auxiliary, 72, 98

COML, 81

Commercial Wireless Services, 136

Common Carrier Voice and Data Communications, 84

Common Challenges, 8

Communications Equipment Manufacturers, 100

Communications Equipment Rental, 101

Communications Flow Diagram, 32

Computer Cables: RJ-45 Connections, 108

Computer Connectors: RS-232, 107

COMT, 81

Contingency Planning, 62

Credible Threat, 51

Critical Mission Communications Requirements, 27

Critical missions, 19

Critical Missions, 20, 21, 22

Current System, 29

DATASTAR, 84

Deliverability, 17

DHS Office of Emergency Communications, 76, 133

Emergency Communications, 137

Emergency Communications Systems, 47, 48, 84

Emergency Communications Systems Comparison, 84

Emergency Managers, 10

Emergency Resource Lists, 67

Emergency Resources, 86

Essential support activities, 19

Essential Support Activities, 24

Essential Support Activity, 25

Family Radio System, 85

Federal Emergency Management Agency, 128

FEMA, 128

FEMA Disaster Emergency Communications, 128

Field Operations Guides, 66, 133

Flexibility, 17

FRS, 85

Fuel Delivery Services, 103

Gap Analysis, 57

General Background Inforrmation, 135

General Mobile Radio System, 85

GETS, 91

GMRS, 85

Government Emergency Telecommunications Service, 91

History, 137

Hot, Warm, Cold Backups, 71

HUGHES NET, 84

ICS, 81

Impact Analysis, 52, 53

Incident Command Communications, 138

Incident Command System, 81, 117

INMARSAT, 84

International Issues, 127

Internet Service Providers, 89

Interoperability, 9, 18, 59, 76, 120, 133, 135, 138, 139, 142, 147

IRIDIUM, 84

Land Mobile Radio, 85

Life-Cycle Affordability, 18

Location-Based Services, 139

Maintainability, 17

Major Challenges, 16

Managing Resources, 80

Military Auxiliary Radio System, 72, 76, 85, 95, 119

Mobile Data Applications, 142

Mobile Emergency Response Support, 128

Morse Code, 114, 119

Multi-Use Radio System, 85

MURS, 85

Mutual Aid Agreements, 47, 68, 71

National Incident Management System, 120

National Interoperability Goal, 59

Networking Technology Assessment, 142

NIFOG, 133

NIMS, 120

Office of Emergency Communications, 58

Planning Overview, 13

Portable Repeaters, 94

Power Generator Rental, 102

Presidential Disaster Declaration, 128

Primary Communications Systems, 41

PSAP, 29, 33, 38, 121, 143

Public Safety, 85, 112, 120, 121, 135, 136, 138, 139, 141, 142, 143, 144, 145, 146, 147, 148

Public Service Answering Point, 29, 38, 121

Radio licensing, 127

Radio Technology Assessment, 144

Reciprocal Licensing, 127

Regional Emergency Communications Coordination Working Group (RECCWG),, 128

Regional Emergency Communications Coordinator, 128

Regulation, 145

Reliability, 17

Restorability, 18

Risk Assessment, 54, 55

Salvation Army Team Emergency Radio Network, 76

Satellite Service Providers, 90

SATERN, 76

Section Emergency Coordinator, 72

Security, 17

Self-Healing Systems, 69

Shared Resources, 96

SHARES, 96

Spectrum, 145

SPOT, 84

Stafford Act, 128

Standard Operating Procedures, 65

Standards, 146

Statewide Interoperability Coordinator, 76

Strategic Planning, 58

Sun Tzu, 3

Tactical Deficiencies, 64

Tactical Gap Analysis, 64

Tactical Planning, 63, 64

Target Capability List, 58

Telecommunications Service Priority, 93

Telephone Frame Room Standards, 110

Telephone Plug Standards, 109

Tower Repair and Climbing Services, 104

Tribal Governments, 128

TSP, 93

U.S. Radio Frequency Allocation Table, 129

Usability, 17

USA-Specific Issues, 128

Vital Communications Needs, 19

Vulnerability Analysis, 56

Wideband/Broadband, 147

WINLINK, 124

Wireless, 84

Wireless Carriers, 88

Wireless LAN, 136, 148

Wireless Priority Service, 92, 125

Wireline, 84

Wireline Carriers, 87

Final Thoughts

> ### *1. Brevity and clarity are essential in emergency communications.*

| PBNY 3-7-41 25M | U. ● NAVAL AIR STATION, KODIAK ● LASKA | |
| Original | NAVAL COMMUNICATIONS | |

Heading	NPC NR 63 F L Z F5L 071830 C8Q TARI O B1	
From:	CINCPAC	Date 7 DEC 41
To:	ALL SHIPS PRESENT AT HAWAIIN AREA.	
Info:	~ U R G E N T ~	
DEFERRED unless otherwise checked	ROUTINE........... PRIORITY......... AIRMAIL.........	

AIRRAID ON REARLHARBOR X THIS IS NO DRILL

> ### 2. Be prepared to use any communication means available.

Photo U.S. Navy/QM2C Tony Evans

This publication is brought to you by

DERA

The International Association for Preparedness and Response

Founded in 1962

Individual and Organizational Partners Welcome

DERA
P.O. Box 797
Longmont, CO 80502 USA

www.disasters.org

Email: **dera@disasters.org**

About DERA

DERA is a Nonprofit Disaster Service and Professional Organization.

Our mission is to foster professional development and networking for our members while providing disaster assistance in these primary areas:

Preparedness - Communications - Logistics

Our members work together as a world-wide network of disaster preparedness specialists, response and recovery teams, trainers, consultants, technical experts, researchers and project managers.

We help disaster victims by improving planning, communications and logistics, conducting training events and community preparedness programs, and by sponsoring emergency response teams.

We sponsor a school awards program that encourages students to study the effects of disasters and to initiate projects that reduce local hazards and improve community preparedness, safety and environmental protection.

As an international professional association, our membership is composed of key leaders in the field of emergency management from around the world, including government officials, volunteers, consultants, business managers, researchers, educators, students and wide range of charitable groups.

Our newsletter, DisasterCom, brings current information about developments in emergency management and reports on the activities of our global membership.

We sponsor research projects and the publication of emergency management guides, case studies, technical assessments, preparedness materials, and an annual peer-reviewed journal.

If you share our vision of commitment and service, we would welcome you as a member.

Please complete a convenient online membership application or contact us for further information.

DERA
P.O. Box 797
Longmont, CO 80502

www.disasters.org

About the Author

Jay Wilson is a native of Asheville, North Carolina. He and his wife, Kathryn, make their home in northern Colorado.

Jay graduated from North Carolina State University with a degree in Political Science and received a Masters in Public Administration from Golden Gate University, followed by postgraduate studies at the University of Southern California and the University of Geneva. His graduate research involved issues of crisis leadership, decision process, and communications reliability.

He studied process management and executive leadership under Dr. W. Edwards Deming and continues to teach and apply the Deming philosophy.

Jay is a Certified Emergency Manager (CEM®) and has held numerous emergency management positions with the federal government. He is a retired Colonel from the United States Air Force, where his duty assignments included communications systems planning and management, maintenance engineering, program development and budgeting, combat support group command and national security emergency preparedness.

Jay has been a licensed Amateur Radio Operator since 1962 and is very active with the Colorado Amateur Radio Emergency Service and numerous amateur radio organizations throughout the world, including the Global Amateur Radio Emergency Communications Committee. He is an active member of the International Association of Emergency Managers, for whom he has been Regional President and member of the Board of Directors. He also serves on the Board of Directors of DERA—The International Association for Preparedness and Response.

Jay has served as on-scene incident commander. HAZMAT operations officer, senior staff trainer and emergency communications group supervisor during many large-scale, multiagency operations, and has deployed in support of more than 120 major incidents.

Jay has taught at the college and university levels, and continues to be an emergency preparedness consultant and trainer for major corporations, public utilities, community organizations and key governmental organizations.

Jay may be reached by email at: b.j.wilson@disasters.org

13144069R00105

Made in the USA
Lexington, KY
27 October 2018